Popular Chinese Cookery

Popular Chinese Cookery

By Alison Burt

Octopus Books

Photographs on pages 47, 50, 79 by courtesy of Syndication International
Photographs on pages 2, 15, 18, 27, 30, 58, 63, 66, 83, 95, 99, 103, 118, 123, by Barry Bullough
Accessories provided by Cheong-Leen Supermarket, London

Frontispiece: A selection of Chinese ingredients and utensils.

First published 1972 by
Octopus Books Limited
59 Grosvenor Street, London W1

ISBN 7064 0130 1

Distributed in USA by Crescent Books
a division of Crown Publishers Inc

Produced by Mandarin Publishers
Printed in Hong Kong

Contents

Weights and Measures

All measurements in this book are based on Imperial weights and measures, with American equivalents given in parenthesis.

Measurements in *weight* in the Imperial and American system are the same.

Measurements in *volume* are different, and the following table shows the equivalents:

Spoon measurements

Imperial	U.S.
1 teaspoon (5ml.)	$1\frac{1}{4}$ teaspoons
1 tablespoon (20ml.)	$1\frac{1}{4}$ tablespoons (abbrev: T)

Level spoon measurements are used in all the recipes.

Liquid measurements

1 Imperial pint	20 fluid ounces
1 American pint	16 fluid ounces
1 American cup	8 fluid ounces

Introduction

The Chinese have always been inscrutable and, to most Westerners, so has their cookery. Although Chinese food is now enjoyed at many Chinese restaurants all over the country, cookery books are few, mainly, I believe, because the Chinese are very bad at writing down their recipes.

Chinese cooks make up their own recipes and seem to know instinctively how much of each ingredient to use. Even with the recipes in this book you can change the quantity of some ingredient or substitute one ingredient for another. You can, in fact, use these recipes as a 'stepping off' point from which you can develop your own initiative and inventiveness. The very essence of Chinese cooking is to use your own personal taste and ideas. Another thing that deters many people from trying to cook Chinese food is that they do not know where to buy the ingredients or if they come across an unusual ingredient, what to use as a substitute if it is unavailable.

Ingredients

Nearly all ingredients for Chinese cooking are available at larger supermarkets or grocery shops and health food stores sometimes stock a range of Chinese groceries. Those items which have to be purchased from shops specializing in Chinese foods are mostly canned or dried so you can stock up when visiting the shop or when ordering by post. If you have the following ingredients in your cupboard in addition to your normal shopping, you will be able to try any of the recipes in this book.

Bamboo Shoot

available canned from larger supermarkets. The sizes vary so use one nearest to that recommended in the recipe. Some cans have the bamboo shoot already sliced which is very convenient.

Bean Sprouts
available canned from larger supermarkets. The sizes vary so use one nearest to that recommended in the recipe. Fresh bean sprouts can be bought from Chinese food stores.

Black Beans (Chinese salted)
available canned from larger supermarkets.

Chow Chow
Canned Chinese preserved fruit, available from Chinese food stores.

Egg Noodles (Chinese dried)
available from larger supermarkets, in packets.

Five-spice Powder
available from Chinese food stores.

Ginger
Fresh ginger can be bought from good greengrocers or supermarkets.

Hoi Sin Sauce
available canned from Chinese food stores.

Lychees
available canned from larger supermarkets. They can sometimes be bought fresh.

Monosodium Glutamate
available from larger supermarkets. This white 'taste powder' is called Ac'cent in Britain and the U.S.A.; Zip in Australia.

Mushrooms
Chinese dried mushrooms are available from Chinese food stores. When fresh mushrooms are needed for a recipe, use small button mushrooms or canned champignons.

Oyster Sauce
available in cans from Chinese food stores.

Sesame Seeds
available from health food shops.

Shark's fin
available, dried, from Chinese food stores.

Soy Sauce
available from larger supermarkets.

Snow Peas
available from greengrocers or Chinese food stores when in season.

Star Anise
available from Chinese food stores.

Transparent Noodles
available from Chinese food stores in packets.

Water Chestnuts
available canned from larger supermarkets.

Preparing the Ingredients

All fresh ingredients should be of good quality and as fresh as possible. The majority of time, when making a Chinese dish, is spent preparing rather than actually cooking the food. Chinese cooking is usually done quickly and the food must be cooked through but remain crisp and succulent. The ingredients are mostly cut up into small pieces and if this is done correctly, the food will become tender more quickly and the dish will look more 'Chinese'! A Chinese cook uses a small chopper for cutting up vegetables, meat, poultry and so on, but a sharp kitchen knife will do these jobs just as well.

Cut *celery* diagonally by slanting the knife to a $45°$ angle and cutting the sticks in $\frac{1}{8}$-$\frac{1}{4}$ inch slices.

Cut *carrot* into wedges by first making a slanting cut across the carrot, then turning it $\frac{1}{3}$ turn away from you and making another slanting cut which comes halfway up the cut surface.

Cut *peppers* into wedges by removing the seeds and membranes, cutting the pepper into strips about $\frac{1}{2}$-$\frac{3}{4}$ inch wide then cutting these diagonally to make triangles. Matchstick strips should be approximately the shape and size of a matchstick.

Cut an *onion* into eighths by placing it on its end and, always cutting downwards, cutting it 0rst in half, then in quarters, and finally into eighths.

Cut *spring onions* (*scallions*) in lengths across, not lengthways. Use about 1 inch of the green.

Cut *water chestnuts* in slices to make small rounds.

Cut *bamboo shoot* as for peppers.

When *crushed garlic* or *finely chopped fresh ginger* are used these ingredients should be almost a pulp.

When a recipe says 'cut *chicken* into eighths', chop it into pieces going right through the bones.

Chicken stock can be substituted with water and a chicken stock cube, except in making soup, when it is important that real stock is used. Frequently chicken dishes use chicken which is boiled first, in which case add a carrot and an onion to the water and use this stock when making the soup.

Beef stock can be substituted with water and beef stock cube except in making soup, when canned beef consommé should be used.

Peanut oil is more widely used in Chinese cooking than other oils. Maize oil, groundnut oil or sunflower seed oil may be used as substitutes, but you should never use olive oil. The oil is hot enough for deep frying when a thermometer reads $375°F$, or when a $\frac{1}{2}$ inch cube of bread browns in the oil in less than a minute.

Meat should be cut across the grain to facilitate the quick cooking procedure.

9

Leftover ingredients will store well in sealed plastic containers in the refrigerator. Dry ingredients should be kept in a cool dry cupboard.

Utensils

The utensil most frequently used in Chinese cooking is a *wok*. This is a large concave pan with a rounded base. It is used for frying (deep and shallow), boiling and simmering, and has the advantage that the food may be pushed to the sides of the pan, allowing the liquid to drain down into the bowl. There is something rather pleasing about using a wok when preparing a Chinese meal, but you can easily use the saucepans and frying pans which you already have in your kitchen. Every Chinese kitchen has a steamer. If you do not own one, use a heatproof bowl or dish and stand it in or over a saucepan of gently simmering water – the result will be the same.
The Chinese use chopsticks for most cooking operations, but unless you are an expert, use a wooden spoon, a perforated kitchen spoon, a fish slice or a pair of kitchen tongs as appropriate. The flavour of Chinese food is very delicate and can easily be tainted with metal, so try to use wooden spoons and china or glass bowls to prevent the food from touching metal as much as possible.

Planning and Preparing a Meal

Planning a Chinese meal is half the fun. The Chinese like to have a variety of dishes for the main course, eating a little of each. I find it easiest to start with soup and then have four dishes to make up the main course, followed by a light dessert. All the recipes in the book state the number of people they will serve but this, of course, will vary according to the number of dishes to be served at a meal. If a recipe serves 4-6 people this means that it will serve four people if four dishes are served; six people if six dishes are served. For your first meal, plan four dishes for the main course, using a variety of ingredients and flavours. One of the dishes will be rice, then perhaps choose one chicken, one pork and one fish, egg or vegetable to make a wide variety. Most of the dishes are cooked on top of the cooker and I find it makes life much easier if I can include one dish which is cooked in the oven. Chinese food may be kept warming for quite a time without spoiling, except for food fried in batter which, naturally, will go soft if kept hot. Make sure that the dishes you choose can all be cooked ahead of time, leaving only one dish at the most which needs last minute cooking. Cover the food with aluminium foil to stop it from becoming dry while being kept warm.

Start preparing the food in good time. Be methodical. Collect all the ingredients together and a selection of saucepans and bowls to put the prepared food in. It is the chopping and cutting of the ingredients that takes time, the actual cooking time is usually very short. If the ingredients are the be marinated, leave them in the marinade until you are ready to cook. Every good Chinese cook washes up as he goes along and I would advise you to do the same; after the meal you will then have a minimum of dishes – even less than with a normal meal.

Garnishes should be prepared with the other ingredients. Sometimes an appropriate garnish is given with a recipe but otherwise use one or more of the following:

Toasted flaked almonds: Place the blanched and flaked almonds in the grill pan under a hot grill. Stir occasionally until golden brown.

Omelette: Beat one egg with salt and pepper. Heat a little oil in a small frying pan and make a thin omelette. Cut into long very thin strips with a sharp knife. Small whole omelettes, about 2 inches in diameter, can also be used.

Spring onion (scallion) flowers: cut a $1\frac{1}{2}$-2 inch length of the green part of a spring onion (scallion). Push out the middle and, using the outside only, snip $\frac{1}{2}$ inch cuts into each end of the spring onion (scallion) about $\frac{1}{8}$-$\frac{1}{4}$ inch apart. Drop each 'flower' into iced water and the snipped ends will curl backwards.

Chopped green spring onion (scallion) top.

Parsley, or Chinese parsley which is not so curly: Chop, or use sprigs.

Watercress, or Chinese watercress, which has thicker leaves: Use in big sprigs.

Transparent noodles: Fry in deep hot oil until puffed up – about 5 seconds. Drain well.

Some menus to try

For 4 people

Tomato Soup with Egg Flower   Raindrop Soup

Fried Rice   Party Fried Rice
Chicken with Lychees   Crisp Skin Chicken
Barbecued Pork with   Shredded Lamb with Onions
    Bean Sprouts   Golden Braised Fish
Shellfish Fritters

Almond Cream with Chow   Gingered Fruits
    Chow

For 5-6 people

Beef and Vegetable Soup	Egg Roll Soup
Boiled Rice	Fried Rice with Crab
Braised Duck with Sweet and Pungent Sauce	Chicken Chop Suey
	Red Roast Pork
Beef Chow Mein	Vegetables with Sweet and Sour Sauce
Mixed Omelette	
Spring Rolls	Wun Tuns
Almond Biscuits	Mow Flower Twists
or	or
Caramel Bananas	Almond Lake with Mandarin Oranges

Entertaining

To entertain your friends Chinese-style is great fun, and since you are preparing and cooking this food, why not serve it in true traditional Chinese fashion? The Chinese are very good at giving feasts – they often have up to 32 courses. They can, however, equally have only three or four, which is much simpler to prepare – especially if you are doing all the cooking yourself.

Plan the menu and prepare the food as suggested in the Introduction. In addition, place small bowls on the table, before the meal begins, with salted nuts, glacé fruits (pineapple, figs, apricots etc.), pickles and any other small delicacies. These appetizers stay on the table throughout the meal, and the guests nibble at them as they please. For a big feast, have about twelve bowls, but for a more modest meal, four to six would be quite adequate.

Set the table, placing a large plate or dish and a small bowl for each person – and a pair of chopsticks (it might be wise to have a fork too!). If soup is to be served, supply a Chinese spoon for each person. This is made of porcelain, which, unlike metal, doesn't get very hot and burn your lips, nor does it taint the very delicate flavour of your carefully prepared soup! All the food is brought to the table in large serving dishes, so put plenty of serving spoons on the table, not forgetting the soup ladle. The Chinese serve the dishes one after the other, but this is not very practical for the Western housewife and so it has become the custom to serve the soup first, followed by all the remaining savoury dishes. The guests help themselves to the food and come back for more as they want it. The meal may last for quite a long time, so it is a good idea to have small food warmers (either electrically heated or using small candles) on the table to keep the food hot.

If you are really going to follow the Chinese style of entertaining, place your guest of honour at the end of the table, facing the door, and arrange the rest of the guests so that the least important is sitting beside the host, who will have his back to the door. Place husbands and wives next to each other, as it is the custom that the ladies depend on their husbands to serve them with food. This usually means that the ladies get all the best and most succulent foods, for who would serve a lady anything but the best!

The soup is eaten from the small bowl, which is then used to put the rice in for the second course. The same plate can be used throughout the meal, but may be changed for the dessert.

Chopsticks are the normal table implements in China. Wooden, plastic of bamboo chopsticks are for everyday use, but for a feast, ivory is preferred. There are many superstitions about chopsticks, one being that it is bad luck to drop them, and another that if you find you have an unmatched pair you will miss your aeroplane, ship or train! So beware – but use them in the correct way and all should be well. Hold the chopsticks just above halfway up. The lower stick should always remain still. It is held between the second and third fingers, and rests on the knuckle of the first finger, kept in place with the thumb. The upper stick is used as a lever for picking up food. Make sure that the ends of the chopsticks are level; hold the upper stick between the tips of the second and third fingers and support it with the ball of the thumb. It takes quite a lot of practice, but if you differentiate between food that is actually picked up between the chopsticks and food that is scooped up on to them, such as rice, you will be more successful.

China Tea. This is served throughout a Chinese meal. It is pale in colour; very scented and extremely refreshing. Keep a special teapot for making China tea and always warm the pot before putting the tea in. Allow 1 teaspoon of tea for each person present, use freshly boiled water and allow the tea leaves to infuse for 3-5 minutes before pouring. Never add milk or sugar to China tea. It is at its best when freshly made, so if you are going to serve it right through a meal, make a fresh pot very frequently.

Chinese Hot-Pot

All the recipes in this book are ideal to serve as part of a feast. For a very special occasion, however, or for something completely different, try serving your guests a Chinese Hot-pot. As well as being delicious to eat, this is also a most attractive meal to present. Chinese fire kettles, especially made for cooking this meal, are available from Chinese stores. They are heated with charcoal and look most impressive on the dining table. You can, however, use a small adjustable spirit burner and place on top an attractive saucepan or fondue pot.

Place the small dishes of appetizers on the table, and on a large platter, arrange a selection of very thin slices of raw meat (fillet steak, lamb's kidney and liver, veal kidney), whole prawns (shrimps), sliced scallops and fish fillets, and bite-size pieces of cooked chicken. Allow a total of about 6 oz. of meat and fish for each person. Also serve rice, fried or boiled, and a crisp salad such as Sesame and Chicken Salad (see recipes pages 106, 108). A selection of Chinese sauces (the recipes of which are given below) should also be served.

Fill the saucepan or fondue pot – or fire kettle – with boiling chicken stock. Place this on the burner and adjust the flame to keep the stock simmering. Add a $\frac{1}{2}$ inch slice of fresh ginger. The guests serve themselves with rice and salad, then select a piece of meat, fish or chicken with chopsticks (or fork!) and dip it in the simmering stock, until it is cooked – about 1-2 minutes. The cooked food is then dipped into a sauce and, finally, eaten. You will find that everyone will soon become their own expert cook.

When all the meat has been cooked and eaten, add to the stock about 2-4 tablespoons of sherry (according to taste) and salt and pepper to taste and serve this to your guests in soup bowls – it is absolutely delicious. A light dessert may follow but this is not normal.

Sauces for Chinese Hot-Pot

Soy and Garlic Sauce: Place $\frac{1}{4}$ pint ($\frac{5}{8}$ cup) of soy sauce in a small saucepan with 2 crushed cloves of garlic. Bring to the boil, simmer for 2 minutes. Serve warm or cold.

Soy and Ginger Sauce: Place $\frac{1}{4}$ pint ($\frac{5}{8}$ cup) of soy sauce in a saucepan with 2 teaspoons of very finely chopped fresh ginger and a pinch of freshly ground black pepper. Bring to the boil and simmer for 2 minutes. Serve warm or cold.

Sweet and Sour Sauce: Place 2 tablespoons ($2\frac{1}{2}$ T) of vinegar and 2 tablespoons ($2\frac{1}{2}$ T) of brown sugar in a small saucepan with 1 tablespoon ($1\frac{1}{4}$ T) of cornflour and salt and pepper to taste. Mix well and stir in $\frac{1}{4}$ pint ($\frac{5}{8}$ cup) of chicken stock and 1 teaspoon of tomato paste. Bring to the boil, stirring constantly, and simmer for 2-3 minutes. Serve warm.

Plum sauce: Plum sauce is available canned from Chinese food stores. To make it at home, mix together 6 tablespoons ($7\frac{1}{2}$ T) of sieved plum jam, 3 tablespoons ($3\frac{3}{4}$ T) of chopped mango chutney, 1 tablespoon ($1\frac{1}{4}$ T) of vinegar, 2 teaspoons of sugar and salt and pepper to taste. Beat well and serve cold.

Hoi Sin Sauce: Available canned from Chinese food stores. Serve cold.

Vinegar and Ginger Sauce: Mix all the following ingredients together thoroughly: 1 tablespoon ($1\frac{1}{4}$ T) of very finely chopped fresh ginger, 1 crushed clove of garlic, 4 tablespoons (5 T) of vinegar, 1 teaspoon of sugar, pinch of monosodium glutamate, 1 teaspoon of tomato paste, salt and pepper to taste. Serve cold.

Soups

Chinese soups have an extremely delicate flavour which
depends almost entirely on the quality of the stock used.
In a Chinese kitchen there is a pot of chicken stock constantly
ready for use. Do not substitute with water and a chicken cube
but try to incorporate a chicken dish in the menu, for which
the chicken has to be boiled. Add a carrot, an onion, a few
peppercorns and the giblets to the cooking water which,
after the chicken has cooked, may be strained and makes a
good stock for soup. Beef stock also must not be substituted
for with water and a beef stock cube. If you have no home
made stock ready, use canned beef consommé.
Always serve Chinese soup piping hot.

BEEF AND VEGETABLE SOUP. PRAWN AND EGG FLOWER SOUP. MUSHROOM SOUP

Mushroom Soup

2 spring onions (scallions)
4 oz. button mushrooms
1½ pints (3¾ cups) chicken
    stock

½ inch slice fresh ginger
1 tablespoon (1¼ T) sherry
salt and pepper

Slice, thinly, the spring onions (scallions) and button mushrooms. Put the stock in a saucepan with the ginger and spring onions. Bring to the boil and simmer, covered, for 20 minutes.

Add the mushrooms and simmer for a further 10 minutes. Remove the ginger. Add the sherry and season to taste. Serve very hot.

Serves 4-6

Prawn (Shrimp) and Egg Flower Soup

2 spring onions (scallions)
1½ pints (3¾ cups) chicken
    stock
½ tablespoon dry sherry
pinch of monosodium
    glutamate

pinch of sugar
1 teaspoon soy sauce
6 oz. (1½ cups) peeled prawns
    (shrimps)
1 egg, well beaten
salt

Chop the spring onions (scallions) finely and put them into a large saucepan with the stock. Bring to the boil and simmer, covered, for 10 minutes.

Add the sherry, monosodium glutamate, sugar, soy sauce and prawns (shrimps). Reheat gently until the prawns (shrimps) are heated through.

Pour in the egg and stir until it separates into shreds. Add salt to taste.

Serve immediately.

Note: King prawns should be deveined and cut in half.

Serves 4-6

Beef and Vegetable Soup

4 oz. beef (topside)
1 tomato
2 spring onions (scallions)
6 water chestnuts
$\frac{1}{2}$ × 8 oz. can bamboo shoot

4 Chinese dried mushrooms
$1\frac{1}{2}$ pints ($3\frac{3}{4}$ cups) beef stock
pinch of monosodium
  glutamate
salt and pepper

Cut the beef into thin strips across the grain of the meat.
Skin the tomato and slice into 4. Slice the spring onions
(scallions), water chestnuts and bamboo shoots into thin strips.
Soak the mushrooms in warm water for 20 minutes, rinse,
squeeze dry and cut into thin strips, discarding the stalks.
Put the stock into a large saucepan and bring to the boil. Add
the beef and simmer for 4-5 minutes. Add the vegetables and
cook for 2 minutes. Add the monosodium glutamate and
season to taste.
Serve very hot.
Serves 4-6

Raindrop Soup

6 water chestnuts
2 spring onions (scallions)
1 tablespoon ($1\frac{1}{4}$ T) sherry
salt and pepper

$1\frac{1}{2}$ pints ($3\frac{3}{4}$ cups) chicken
  stock
6 oz. ($1\frac{1}{2}$ cups) diced cooked
  chicken

Slice the water chestnuts and slice the spring onions
(scallions) finely. Put these into a saucepan with the chicken
stock and the chicken. Bring to the boil and simmer, covered,
for 15 minutes.
Add the sherry and season to taste.
Serve very hot.
Serves 4-6

Wun Tun Soup

Either buy ready made wun tun skins from a shop which specializes in Chinese groceries, or make your own, using ¼ of the quantities in the recipe given on page 114.

1½ pints (3¾ cups) chicken
   stock
salt and pepper
4 oz. (1 cup) chopped cooked
   chicken
4 oz. (1 cup) peeled prawns
   (shrimps)

2 spring onions (scallions)
8 wun tun skins
1 egg white
snipped green tops of spring
   onions (scallions)

Put the stock in a large saucepan and heat slowly until boiling, seasoning to taste.

Chop the chicken, prawns (shrimps) and spring onions (scallions) very very finely and mix them together. Place some of this filling on each wun tun skin, moisten the edges with a little egg white and fold over like a small turnover. Press the edges together well.

Drop the wun tuns into the boiling stock and cook for about 10 minutes.

Serve sprinkled with snipped green spring onion (scallion) tops.

Serves 8

Tomato Soup with Egg Flower

4 tomatoes
1 onion
1 tablespoon (1¼ T) oil
1½ pints (3¾ cups) chicken stock

pinch of monosodium
   glutamate
salt and pepper
1 egg, beaten

Skin and cut the tomatoes and cut the onions into eighths. Heat the oil in a large saucepan. Add the tomatoes and onion

and fry for 5 minutes or until softened but not browned.
Pour off the excess oil and add the stock, salt and pepper and
monosodium glutamate. Bring to the boil and simmer for
30 minutes.
Add the egg slowly, stirring constantly until it separates into
shreds.
Serve immediately.
Serves 4-6

Shark's Fin Soup

4 oz. dried shark's fin
1 tablespoon ($1\frac{1}{4}$ T) peanut oil
1 teaspoon fresh ginger
2 spring onions (scallions)
4 oz. (1 cup) crab meat
$\frac{1}{2}$ × 5 oz. can bamboo shoot
1 tablespoon ($1\frac{1}{4}$ T) sherry

2 pints (5 cups) chicken stock
1 tablespoon ($1\frac{1}{4}$ T) cornflour
  (cornstarch)
1 teaspoon soy sauce
$\frac{1}{2}$ teaspoon monosodium
  glutamate
salt and pepper to taste

Wash the shark's fin and soak it for 6-8 hours or overnight.
Place the shark's fin in a large saucepan and cover with fresh
water. Bring to the boil, cover and simmer for 2-3 hours.
Drain.
Chop the ginger very finely and chop the spring onions
(scallions). Chop the crab meat and slice the bamboo shoot
finely.
Heat the oil in a saucepan, add the ginger and spring onions
and fry for 2-3 minutes. Add the sherry, chicken stock and
shark's fin. Bring to the boil and simmer for 20 minutes.
Mix the cornflour (cornstarch), soy sauce, monosodium
glutamate and seasonings and add to the pan. Simmer, stirring,
for 3-4 minutes. Add the crab meat and bamboo shoot and
reheat. Serve very hot.
Serves 4-6

Egg Roll Soup

8 oz. (2 cups) minced (ground) cold cooked pork
salt and pepper
1 teaspoon soy sauce
pinch of monosodium glutamate
1 teaspoon cornflour (cornstarch)
1 tablespoon (1¼ T) oil
2 eggs
flour and water for paste
2 carrots, sliced
1½ pints (3¾ cups) beef stock

Mix the pork, salt and pepper, soy sauce, monosodium glutamate and cornflour (cornstarch) together thoroughly. Beat the eggs with salt and pepper. Heat half the oil in a 6 inch pan, add half the egg mixture and make a small omelette. Heat the remaining oil and make another omelette with the remaining egg. Do not fold the omelettes.
Spread a thin layer of the pork mixture on each omelette and roll it up like a Swiss roll. Seal with a thick paste of flour and water.
Place the rolls in a pudding basin with the carrot. Put the basin in a large saucepan with water coming halfway up the side of the basin. Bring to the boil and simmer, covered, for 30 minutes.
Put the stock in a large saucepan and bring it to the boil. Pour it into individual soup bowls.
Cut the egg rolls into diagonal slices about ¾ inch wide and add them to the bowls with the carrot.
Serve immediately.
Serves 4-6

Fish

Fish is widely eaten in China, especially in the coastal areas. The fish used in Chinese cooking should always be very fresh and this is considered so important that in Chinese food stores the fish are often alive, swimming in large barrels. When you buy your fish, ask your fishmonger for some fish heads, so that you can cook them in simmering water with a bay leaf, 6 peppercorns and half an onion to make your own delicious fish stock.

At least one fish dish is usually included in the main course if you are entertaining Chinese style. Frequently this is shellfish, as the delicate flavours of prawns (shrimps), scallops, crab and so on lend themselves to Chinese cooking. If you are able to buy 'green' or uncooked prawns use these in preference to the ready cooked ones.

Fish Rolls with Walnuts

This dish makes an ideal appetizer, either to begin the meal or served with drinks beforehand.

2 large fish fillets (John Dory, Flounder, Plaice or Sole)
2 spring onions (scallions)
$\frac{1}{2}$ teaspoon salt
$\frac{1}{2}$ teaspoon sugar
$\frac{1}{2}$ teaspoon cornflour (cornstarch)
1 teaspoon soy sauce
1 teaspoon dry sherry
1 egg
2 oz. ($\frac{1}{2}$ cup) walnuts, very finely chopped or ground
2 × 1 oz. slices cooked ham
8 wooden cocktail sticks
oil for deep frying

Cut the fillets into quarters, making 8 even-sized pieces.
Chop the spring onions (scallions) finely, mix with salt, sugar, cornflour (cornstarch), soy sauce, sherry and egg and beat together well.
Dip the fish pieces in the egg mixture and then in the walnuts.
Cut each slice of ham in quarters and lay a quarter on each piece of fish. Roll up and secure with a cocktail stick.
Deep fry in hot oil until golden. Drain well on absorbent kitchen paper.
Serve very hot.
Serves 4-6

Fish in Sweet and Sour Sauce

1 lb. fish fillets
1 carrot
1 green pepper
2 sticks celery
3 tomatoes
3 tablespoons (3¾ T) peanut oil
4 tablespoons (5 T) vinegar
4 tablespoons (5 T) sugar
1 teaspoon very finely
chopped fresh ginger
½ teaspoon salt
½ tablespoon cornflour
(cornstarch)

Skin the fish and cut it into bite-sized pieces. Cut the carrot and pepper into matchstick strips. Cut the celery diagonally. Drop the prepared vegetables into boiling water and simmer for 5 minutes. Drain.
Skin the tomatoes, remove seeds and chop roughly. Heat the oil in a small pan and fry the fish until cooked, about 5-7 minutes. Remove the fish and drain.
Pour off excess oil, add the vinegar, sugar, ginger, salt, cornflour (cornstarch), all the vegetables and ¼ pint (⅝ cup) of water. Bring to the boil, stirring, add the fish and simmer for 2 minutes.
Serve in a heated dish.
Serves 4-6

Golden Braised Fish

1 × 2 lb. whole fish (Bream,
Bass or Snapper are
suitable)
salt
plain flour
4 Chinese dried mushrooms
4 spring onions (scallions)
oil for frying
1 teaspoon very finely
chopped fresh ginger
½ pint (1¼ cups) fish stock or
water
2 tablespoons (2½ T) soy sauce
1 tablespoon (1¼ T) sherry
1 teaspoon salt
6 water chestnuts
2 cloves garlic, crushed
1 clove star anise
1 teaspoon sugar

Clean the fish, leaving on the head and tail. Wipe inside and out with kitchen paper. Make 2 gashes on each side, in the thickest part. Sprinkle with salt and coat in flour. Soak the mushrooms in warm water for 20 minutes, rinse, squeeze dry and discard stalks. Cut the mushrooms into strips and the spring onions (scallions) into ½ inch lengths. Slice the water chestnuts.

Heat a little oil in a large frying pan and, when hot, fry the fish on both sides until golden. Pour off excess oil and add the mushrooms, spring onions (scallions), ginger, stock, soy sauce, sherry, salt, water chestnuts, garlic, star anise and sugar. Cover the pan, bring to the boil and simmer for about 30 minutes, turning the fish once.

Serve on a large heated plate with the sauce poured over.

Serves 4-6

Sesame Fish

Sesame fish can also be served as a delicious appetizer.

1 lb. fish fillets
1 teaspoon very finely
   chopped fresh ginger
1 onion
2 tablespoons (2½ T) dry
   sherry
½ teaspoon salt
pinch of pepper

1 teaspoon sugar
1 oz. (¼ cup) cornflour
   (cornstarch)
1 oz. (¼ cup) plain flour
1 egg
sesame seeds
oil for deep frying

Skin the fish and cut into bite-sized pieces. Chop the onion finely and mix together in a bowl with the ginger, sherry, salt, pepper and sugar. Add the fish pieces and marinate for 10 minutes, stirring occasionally. Drain.

Sift the cornflour and flour into a bowl. Add egg, 3 table-spoons water and mix well. Dip fish in this batter, then in sesame seeds. Deep fry in hot oil until crisp and golden. Serve hot.

Serves 4-6

Crisp Skin Fish

4 whiting
4 oz. (1 cup) peeled prawns (shrimps)
4 Chinese dried mushrooms
1 spring onion (scallion)
1 teaspoon very finely chopped fresh ginger
salt
1 egg yolk
cornflour (cornstarch)

oil for frying
1 tablespoon ($1\frac{1}{4}$ T) vinegar
1 tablespoon ($1\frac{1}{4}$ T) sugar
2 tablespoons ($2\frac{1}{2}$ T) Chinese black beans
1 tablespoon ($1\frac{1}{4}$ T) cornflour (cornstarch)
$\frac{1}{4}$ pint ($\frac{5}{8}$ cup) fish stock or water
1 tablespoon ($1\frac{1}{4}$ T) soy sauce

Clean the whiting, leaving on the heads and tails. Chop the prawns (shrimps) and spring onions (scallions). Soak the mushrooms for 20 minutes, rinse, squeeze dry, and chop, discarding the stalks.

Mix the prawns (shrimps), mushrooms, spring onions (scallions) and ginger and stuff each fish with this mixture. Sew up the openings. Rub salt into gashes cut on both sides of each fish in the thickest part.

Beat the egg yolk with 1 teaspoon of water and brush over the fish. When nearly dry, rub over the cornflour (cornstarch). Heat about 2 inches of oil in a pan and fry the fish, turning once. When cooked, drain on absorbent paper. Keep hot.

Place all the remaining ingredients in a small saucepan with salt to taste. Bring to the boil, stirring constantly, and simmer for 2-3 minutes. Place the fish on a hot serving plate, pour the sauce over and serve.

Serves 4-8

Pineapple Fish

1 lb. fish fillet (haddock or snapper) or 2 × 7 oz. cans tuna

4 oz. (1 cup) self raising (all purpose) flour

pinch of salt

1 egg

$\frac{1}{4}$ pint ($\frac{5}{8}$ cup) water

pinch of monosodium glutamate

4 pineapple rings

2 tablespoons (2$\frac{1}{2}$ T) soft brown sugar

1 tablespoon (1$\frac{1}{4}$ T) cornflour (cornstarch)

2 tablespoons (2$\frac{1}{2}$ T) vinegar

1 tablespoon (1$\frac{1}{4}$ T) soy sauce

1 teaspoon very finely chopped fresh ginger

$\frac{1}{4}$ pint ($\frac{5}{8}$ cup) syrup from canned pineapple

salt to taste

toasted flaked almonds for garnish

oil for deep frying

Skin the fish and cut into bite-sized pieces or drain the tuna and break into bite-sized pieces.

Sift the flour and salt together into a mixing bowl. Make a well in the centre, add the egg and mix with a little flour, using a wooden spoon. Gradually add the water, then the flour, and beat until the batter is smooth. Beat in the monosodium glutamate.

Chop the pineapple roughly. Mix together the brown sugar, cornflour (cornstarch), vinegar, soy sauce, ginger, pineapple syrup, salt and $\frac{1}{4}$ pint ($\frac{5}{8}$ cup) of water. Bring to the boil, stirring, and boil for 2–3 minutes.

Dip the fish pieces in batter and fry in deep hot oil until crisp and golden. Drain on absorbent kitchen paper. Add the pineapple pieces to the sauce and reheat.

Sprinkle the fish with the toasted flaked almonds and serve in a hot serving bowl with the sauce poured over.

Serves 4-6

Butterfly Prawns with Celery and Mushrooms

1 lb. king prawns (shrimps), peeled
2 oz. ($\frac{1}{2}$ cup) self raising (all purpose) flour
pinch of salt
4 fl. oz. ($\frac{1}{2}$ cup) water
$\frac{1}{2}$ teaspoon vinegar
4 Chinese dried mushrooms
4 sticks celery
1 tablespoon ($1\frac{1}{4}$ T) peanut oil
1 clove garlic, crushed
2 teaspoons soy sauce
1 tablespoon ($1\frac{1}{4}$ T) dry sherry
salt and pepper to taste
oil for deep frying

Remove the dark vein from the back of each prawn (shrimp) and cut nearly, but not quite, in half lengthways. Open them out like butterflies and press open between the palms of your hands.

Sift the flour and salt into a bowl and mix in water and vinegar to make a smooth batter.

Soak mushrooms in warm water for 20 minutes, rinse, squeeze dry, and slice thinly, discarding the stalks. Slice the celery diagonally.

Heat the oil in a small saucepan and add the garlic, mushrooms, and celery. Fry, stirring, for 3 minutes. Add the sherry, soy sauce, seasonings and 4 tablespoons of water.

Dip the prawns (shrimps) into the batter and deep fry in hot oil until golden. Drain on absorbent kitchen paper. Reheat the sauce.

Serve immediately, with the sauce poured over the prawns (shrimps).

Serves 4-6

Prawn (Shrimp) Chop Suey

8 oz. (2 cups) peeled prawns (shrimps)
4 Chinese dried mushrooms
1 × 16 oz. can bean sprouts
$\frac{1}{2}$ × 8 oz. can bamboo shoot
8 water chestnuts
pinch of salt
1 tablespoon ($1\frac{1}{4}$ T) soy sauce
1 clove garlic, crushed
1 teaspoon sugar
1 tablespoon ($1\frac{1}{4}$ T) dry sherry

½ tablespoon cornflour
  (cornstarch)

2 oz. (½ cup) blanched toasted
  almonds

Prepare the prawns (shrimps), cutting the large ones in half. Soak the mushrooms in warm water for 20 minutes, rinse, squeeze dry and slice, discarding the stalks. Rinse the bean sprouts under running cold water. Drain. Cut the bamboo shoot and water chestnuts into matchstick strips.

Mix the cornflour (cornstarch), salt, soy sauce, garlic, sugar, sherry, vegetables and 4 tablespoons of water in a small saucepan. Bring to the boil and simmer slowly, stirring, for 2-3 minutes. Stir in the prawns (shrimps), cover the pan and reheat gently. Serve on a heated serving dish topped with the almonds.

Note Toast the almonds by heating under a hot grill, stirring occasionally until golden.

Serves 4-6

Prawn (Shrimp) Balls

4 oz. (1 cup) self raising
  (all purpose) flour
1 egg
¼ pint (⅝ cup) water
pinch of salt
1 lb. peeled king prawns
  (shrimps)

2 tablespoons (2½ T) cornflour
  (cornstarch)
½ teaspoon salt
½ teaspoon white pepper
pinch monosodium glutamate
peanut oil for deep frying
parsley sprigs for garnish

Sift the flour and salt into a bowl. Make a well in the centre and add the egg. Using a wooden spoon, mix the flour into the egg, add half the water and continue mixing, drawing in the flour. Beat thoroughly and stir in remaining water. Cut the prawns (shrimps) into chunks about 1 inch across. Mix the cornflour (cornstarch) with the remaining salt, pepper and monosodium glutamate. Coat the prawn (shrimp) pieces in seasoned cornflour (cornstarch). Dip the prawns (shrimps) in batter and fry in deep, hot oil until crisp and golden. Drain well on absorbent kitchen paper.

Serve hot, garnished with sprigs of parsley.

Serves 4-6

PINEAPPLE FISH (*Photograph: John West*)

Sweet and Sour Prawns (Shrimps)

8 oz. (2 cups) peeled prawns (shrimps)
1 tablespoon (1¼ T) sherry
salt and pepper
1 onion
1 green pepper
1 tablespoon (1¼ T) peanut oil
½ × 15 oz. can pineapple chunks

1 tablespoon (1¼ T) cornflour (cornstarch)
1 tablespoon (1¼ T) soy sauce
¼ pint (⅝ cup) vinegar
4 tablespoons (5 T) brown sugar

Place the prawns (shrimps) in a bowl with the sherry and seasonings and marinate for 1 hour.
Slice the onion and cut the pepper into wedges. Put the oil in a small saucepan, add the vegetables, and fry gently until softened. Add the pineapple.
Mix together the cornflour (cornstarch), soy sauce, vinegar and sugar and add these to the saucepan. Bring to the boil, stirring constantly, and simmer for 2-3 minutes. Add the prawns (shrimps) and sherry and reheat.
Serve in a heated bowl.
Serves 4-6

Shellfish Fritters

1 lb. (4 cups) mixed prepared shellfish (prawns (shrimps), crab, lobster, scallops)
1 clove garlic, crushed
salt and pepper
3 eggs
2 oz. (½ cup) plain flour
3 Chinese dried mushrooms
½ × 5 oz. can bamboo shoot
8 water chestnuts

1 teaspoon very finely chopped fresh ginger
2 sticks celery
½ tablespoon soy sauce
½ tablespoon dry sherry
¼ pint (⅝ cup) chicken stock
½ tablespoon cornflour (cornstarch)
pinch of sugar
oil for deep frying

PRAWN BALLS AND VEGETABLES WITH SWEET AND SOUR SAUCE (*Photograph: American Rice Council*)

Chop the shellfish and mix with garlic, salt and pepper. Beat the eggs and then beat in the flour and shellfish mixture. Mix together thoroughly.

Soak the mushrooms in warm water for 20 minutes, rinse, squeeze dry and slice, discarding the stalks. Cut the bamboo shoot into matchstick strips and slice the water chestnuts. Cut the celery in diagonal slices.

Mix together in a small saucepan, the ginger, soy sauce, sherry, stock, cornflour (cornstarch) and sugar. Bring to the boil, stirring. Add the vegetables and simmer for 2-3 minutes.

Heat the oil and drop in teaspoons of the shellfish mixture. Deep fry until golden and crisp. Drain well on absorbent kitchen paper.

Serve immediately, in a hot serving bowl, with the sauce poured over.

Serves 4-6

Shellfish and Cucumber Salad

12 oz. (3 cups) mixed shellfish (prawns (shrimps), crab, lobster, scallops etc.)
1 cucumber
1 teaspoon very finely chopped fresh ginger
1 tablespoon ($1\frac{1}{4}$ T) soy sauce
1 tablespoon ($1\frac{1}{4}$ T) vinegar
3 tablespoons ($3\frac{3}{4}$ T) oil
1 teaspoon sugar
salt and pepper
lettuce or Chinese cabbage if available.

Cut the shellfish into bite-sized pieces. Peel the cucumber and cut into matchstick strips. Mix together the ginger, soy sauce, vinegar, oil and sugar. Add the shellfish and toss them all together.

Arrange a bed of lettuce leaves in a serving bowl. Put the cucumber on top in a ring and place the shellfish inside the ring of cucumber. Chill before serving.

Serves 4

Prawns (Shrimps) with Vegetable.

1 lb. prawns (shrimps), peeled
1 red pepper
2 sticks celery
2 Chinese dried mushrooms
2 spring onions (scallions)
6 water chestnuts
1 tablespoon ($1\frac{1}{4}$ T) cornflour
  (cornstarch)
1 tablespoon ($1\frac{1}{4}$ T) soy sauce
pinch of sugar

1 tablespoon ($1\frac{1}{4}$ T) peanut oil
$\frac{1}{2}$ teaspoon very finely
  chopped fresh ginger
1 clove garlic, crushed
$\frac{1}{2}$ teaspoon salt
2 pineapple rings, chopped
  (optional)
$\frac{1}{2}$ pint ($1\frac{1}{4}$ cups) chicken stock
1 oz. ($\frac{1}{4}$ cup) flaked toasted
  almonds

Prepare the prawns (shrimps). If using large prawns (shrimps),
devein them and cut them in half.

Cut the pepper in matchstick strips and slice the celery
diagonally. Soak the mushrooms in warm water for 20 minutes,
rinse and squeeze dry, discarding the stalks, and slice. Cut the
spring onions (scallions) in $\frac{1}{2}$ inch pieces and slice the water
chestnuts. Mix the cornflour (cornstarch) with soy sauce,
sugar and 2 tablespoons of water.

Heat the oil and add the ginger, garlic and salt. Add the
prepared vegetables, pineapple and stock. Bring to the
boil and simmer, stirring, for 5 minutes. Add the cornflour
mixture and cook, stirring, for 2-3 minutes. Add the prawns
and allow just to heat through.

Serve in a hot serving dish, scattered with flaked toasted
almonds.

Note: Toast flaked almonds by heating under a hot grill,
stirring occasionally, until golden.

Serves 4-6

Scallops with Bamboo Shoot

This dish can also be served as an appetizer.

12 oz. scallops
2 teaspoons cornflour
  (cornstarch)
2 teaspoons soy sauce
1 teaspoon sugar
1 × 5 oz. can bamboo shoot
2 sticks celery

1 pineapple ring
1 onion
2 tablespoons (2½ T) peanut oil
salt
¼ pint (⅝ cup) fish stock or
  water

Cut the scallops in half. Mix together the cornflour (cornstarch), soy sauce and sugar with 1 tablespoon of water. Cut the bamboo shoot into thin strips, the celery into diagonal slices, the pineapple into wedges and the onion into eighths. Heat the oil in a frying pan and fry the scallops for 3-5 minutes. Remove and drain.

Add the bamboo shoot, celery, pineapple and onion to the pan and fry for 3 minutes. Add the salt and stock, bring to the boil and simmer for 2-3 minutes. Stir the cornflour (cornstarch) mixture and stir it into the pan. Simmer for another 2 minutes. Pour the hot sauce over the scallops and serve.
Serves 4-6

Meat

Pork is the meat most commonly eaten in China, except where religion forbids it, when beef is eaten instead. Use the best possible cuts of meat and always slice it across the grain which helps to make it more tender for the Chinese-style quick cooking. Although the meat may be expensive, a little goes a long way, and each dish works out to be quite economical.

Crispy Pork

This dish is delicious served with Sweet and Sour Vegetables (see page 105).

1 lb. lean pork
2 tablespoons (2½ T) soy sauce
1 tablespoon (1¼ T) sugar
1 clove star anise
1 tablespoon (1¼ T) sherry
 (optional)
pinch of monosodium
 glutamate

4 oz. (1 cup) self raising (all
 purpose) flour
pinch of salt
1 egg
oil for frying

Cut the pork into 1 inch cubes. Put them in a saucepan with ¾ pint (approx. 2 cups) of water, soy sauce, sugar, star aniseed, sherry and monosodium glutamate. Simmer until tender, about 45 minutes. Drain well.

Sift the flour and salt into a bowl. Make a well in the centre, drop in the egg and mix with a wooden spoon, gradually bringing in the flour from around the edge. Add ¼ pint (⅝ cup) of water gradually, beating continually. Add the pork pieces and stir to coat in batter.

Heat oil in a frying pan and deep fry the coated pork pieces until crisp and golden. Drain well on absorbent kitchen paper. Serve as soon as possible.

Serves 4-6

Barbecued Pork with Bean Sprout

1 lb. lean pork
1 spring onion (scallion)
2 × ¼ inch slices fresh ginger
4 tablespoons (5 T) hoi sin or soy sauce
2 tablespoons (2½ T) dry sherry
1 clove garlic, crushed

2 tablespoons (2½ T) honey
1 tablespoon (1¼ T) peanut oil
1 teaspoon very finely chopped fresh ginger
½ teaspoon salt
1 × 16 oz. can bean sprouts
1 teaspoon sugar

Cut pork into strips, 2 inch × 1 inch × 1 inch. Chop onion finely. Mix together, in an oblong dish, the ginger, soy sauce, sherry, spring onion (scallion) and garlic. Add the pork strips, coat with marinade and leave for 4-6 hours, stirring occasionally.

Drain the pork and rub it with honey. Place on a greased rack in a roasting pan over 1 inch of water. Cook for 25 minutes at 350°F, Mark 4. Slice into thin pieces.

Heat the oil in a saucepan, add the chopped ginger and salt and fry for 2 minutes. Drain the bean sprouts, rinse in cold running water, drain again and add to the saucepan with 1 tablespoon of water and the sugar. Heat gently, stirring until well mixed. Add the pork, cover, and heat through.

Serves 4-6

Pork and Mushroom Balls with Vegetables

4 Chinese dried mushrooms
¾ lb. minced (ground) pork
cornflour (cornstarch)
½ tablespoon dry sherry
salt, pepper
1 onion, sliced
2 sticks celery

4 tomatoes
6 water chestnuts, sliced
½ × 16 oz. can bean sprouts
2 tablespoons (2½ T) peanut oil
¼ pint (⅝ cup) chicken stock
1 tablespoon (1¼ T) soy sauce

Soak the mushrooms in warm water for 20 minutes, rinse, squeeze dry and chop finely, discarding the stalks. Mix thoroughly the pork, mushrooms, cornflour (cornstarch), sherry, salt and pepper. Form the mixture into small balls and roll them in cornflour (cornstarch).

Cut the celery diagonally. Skin, deseed and slice the tomatoes. Drain bean sprouts, rinse in running water and drain again. Heat the oil in a saucepan and fry the pork and mushroom balls until golden. Cover and cook very gently for a further 6-8 minutes. Remove and add the onion, celery, tomatoes and water chestnuts. Fry, stirring, for 5 minutes.

Pour off any oil and add the chicken stock blended with 1 tablespoon cornflour (cornstarch), salt and soy sauce. Bring to the boil, stirring, and simmer for 2-3 minutes. Add the bean sprouts and pork and mushroom balls and reheat.

Serves 4-6

Pork Balls

$\frac{3}{4}$ lb. spring or shoulder
  (picnic shoulder) pork
8 water chestnuts
1 onion
$\frac{1}{2}$ oz. preserved ginger (in
  syrup)

$\frac{1}{2}$ tablespoon soy sauce
salt and pepper
cornflour (cornstarch)
oil for deep frying

Mince or chop very finely, the pork, water chestnuts, onion and ginger. Add the soy sauce and combine thoroughly. Season Form the mixture into small balls and roll them in cornflour (cornstarch). Deep fry in hot oil until they float to the top. Drain well on absorbent kitchen paper.

Serve hot, either on their own or with fried rice.

Serves 4-6

PORK BALLS ON FRIED CABBAGE. PORK WITH SWEET AND PUNGENT SAUCE

Pork with Bean Sprouts and Almonds

$\frac{3}{4}$ lb. shoulder or spring
   (picnic shoulder) pork
1 × 16 oz. can bean sprouts
2 oz. ($\frac{1}{2}$ cup) blanched almonds
1 tablespoon ($1\frac{1}{4}$ T) soy sauce
2 tablespoon ($2\frac{1}{2}$ T) chicken
   stock

1 teaspoon sugar
2 tablespoons ($2\frac{1}{2}$ T) peanut oil
2 spring onions (scallions),
   thinly sliced
1 pineapple ring, chopped
salt and pepper

Cut the pork into $\frac{1}{2}$ inch cubes. Drain the bean sprouts, rinse
in cold running water and drain again. Halve the almonds.
Mix together the soy sauce, chicken stock and sugar.
Heat the oil in a frying pan and fry the pork, stirring, until
it changes colour. Add the almonds and spring onions
(scallions) and fry for 3-4 minutes. Pour off any oil. Add all the
other ingredients, including the bean sprouts. Combine
thoroughly, cover the pan and cook for 2 minutes.
Serves 4-6

PORK WITH BEAN SPROUTS AND ALMONDS (*Photograph: American Rice Council*)

Pork with Chicken and Vegetables

½ lb. spring or shoulder
   (picnic shoulder) pork
¼ lb. chicken
1 small red pepper
1 onion
2 sticks celery
6 water chestnuts
1 × 5 oz. can bamboo shoot
2 oz. button mushrooms

2 tablespoons (2½ T) peanut oil
1 tablespoon (1¼ T) soy sauce
¼ pint (⅝ cup) chicken stock
salt and pepper
1 tablespoon (1¼ T) cornflour
   (cornstarch)
4 oz. Chinese dried egg
   noodles

Cut the pork and the chicken into thin strips. Cut the pepper into matchstick strips and the onion into eighths. Slice the celery diagonally and the water chestnuts and bamboo shoot into thin slices. Wipe and slice the mushrooms.

Heat the oil in a saucepan and fry the pork and chicken until they change colour, stirring constantly. Add the vegetables and fry, stirring, for 2-3 minutes. Pour off excess oil. Add the soy sauce, stock and seasonings and simmer for 5-7 minutes. Mix the cornflour (cornstarch) with a little water, add to the pan and simmer, stirring, for 2-3 minutes.

Cook the noodles in boiling salted water for 15 minutes. Drain. Serve with sauce poured over the noodles.

Serves 4-6

Sweet and Sour Pork with Lychees

1 lb. spring or shoulder (picnic shoulder) pork
3 tablespoons (3¾ T) soy sauce
1 tablespoon (1¼ T) dry sherry
1 teaspoon very finely chopped fresh ginger
pinch of monosodium glutamate
1 oz. (¼ cup) plain flour
1 oz. (¼ cup) cornflour (cornstarch)
pinch of salt
2 eggs, beaten
oil for deep frying
½ red pepper
½ green pepper
2 apples
1 tablespoon (1¼ T) brown sugar
¼ pint (⅝ cup) syrup from canned lychees
2 tablespoons (2½ T) vinegar
4 spring onions (scallions), finely chopped
1 × 11 oz. can lychees, drained
extra 1 tablespoon (1¼ T) cornflour (cornstarch)
extra 1 tablespoon (1¼ T) soy sauce
salt to taste

Cut the pork into 1 inch cubes. Mix together in a bowl the soy sauce, sherry, ginger and monosodium glutamate. Add the pork, stir to coat and marinate for 1-2 hours.
Sift the plain flour, cornflour (cornstarch) and salt into a bowl. Add the eggs gradually, beating well, to make a smooth batter. Coat the pork cubes in batter and deep fry in hot oil until golden. Drain on absorbent kitchen paper and keep hot.
Cut the peppers into wedges. Peel, core and quarter the apples. Mix with all the remaining ingredients in a small saucepan. Bring to the boil, stirring constantly, and simmer for 2-3 minutes.
Put the pork on a heated serving dish and pour the sauce over. Serve as soon as possible.
Serves 4-6

Pork with Sweet and Pungent Sauce

1 lb. shoulder or spring (picnic shoulder) pork
4 tablespoons (5 T) soy sauce
2 cloves star anise
1 tablespoon (1¼ T) brown sugar
¾ pint (approx. 2 cups) chicken stock
1 carrot
1 small red or green pepper
4 pineapple rings
2 tablespoons (2½ T) brown sugar
2 tablespoons (2½ T) vinegar
1 teaspoon very finely chopped fresh ginger
1 clove garlic, crushed
1 tablespoon tomato paste
½ teaspoon salt
1 tablespoon (1¼ T) dry sherry
1 tablespoon (1¼ T) cornflour

Cut pork into long thin strips. Mix marinade of soy sauce, star aniseed, brown sugar and chicken stock. Marinate the pork for about 2 hours. Pour the pork and marinade into a saucepan, bring to the boil, stirring constantly, simmer for 20 minutes and drain.
Cut the carrot and pepper into wedges, drop into a saucepan of boiling water and simmer for 5 minutes. Drain. Cut pineapple rings into eighths. Place pork, vegetables, pineapple, ¼ pint water and all remaining ingredients into a saucepan. Bring to the boil, stirring constantly and simmer for 3-4 minutes.
Serves 4-6

Red Roast Pork

1 lb. pork fillet
1 tablespoon (1¼ T) hoi sin sauce
1 teaspoon five-spice powder
1 tablespoon (1¼ T) soy sauce
½ tablespoon soft brown sugar
1 clove garlic, crushed
1 teaspoon very finely chopped fresh ginger
peanut oil

56

Trim the pork but leave it in one piece. Mix together all the remaining ingredients except the oil and combine them thoroughly.

Place the meat in a dish, brush it with oil and then coat it in sauce. Marinate the pork for 1-2 hours.

Spoon more oil over the pork, place on a rack in a roasting pan and roast in a hot oven (425°F, Mark 6) for 10 minutes. Reduce the oven temperature to moderate (350°F, Mark 4) for 30-35 minutes.

Cut the fillet in slices diagonally and serve on a hot plate.

Note: Other cuts of pork may be roasted with this sauce. Adjust the roasting time, allowing 35 minutes per pound.
Serves 4-6

Shredded Spiced Pork

1 lb. lean pork (shoulder or leg)
4 Chinese dried mushrooms
6 water chestnuts, sliced
2 spring onions (scallions), chopped
1 egg
2 oz. ($\frac{1}{2}$ cup) cornflour (cornstarch)

oil for deep frying
1 tablespoon ($1\frac{1}{4}$ T) peanut oil
1 teaspoon soy sauce
2 teaspoons hoi sin sauce
$\frac{1}{4}$ teaspoon cayenne pepper
$\frac{1}{2}$ teaspoon salt
1 oz. transparent noodles for garnish

Cut the pork into thin slices. Soak mushrooms in warm water, rinse, squeeze dry and slice thinly, discarding the stalks.

Beat the egg and cornflour (cornstarch) together. Coat the pork in batter and deep fry in hot oil until it is beginning to brown.

Heat the peanut oil in a frying pan. Add the mushrooms, water chestnuts, spring onions (scallions), soy sauce, hoi sin sauce, cayenne pepper, salt and fried pork. Cook for 5 minutes, stirring constantly.

Fry noodles in deep hot oil for about 15 seconds.

Serve pork on a heated dish, topped with the noodles.
Serves 4-6

Sweet and Sour Spareribs

Sweet and sour spareribs should be eaten with the fingers. Supply finger bowls filled with cold water.

3 lb. pork spareribs
$\frac{1}{2}$ pint (1$\frac{1}{4}$ cups) vinegar
3 oz. ($\frac{3}{4}$ cup) cornflour (cornstarch)
2 tablespoons (2$\frac{1}{2}$ T) honey
1 tablespoon (1$\frac{1}{4}$ T) soy sauce
oil for frying
$\frac{1}{4}$ pint ($\frac{5}{8}$ cup) syrup from

canned pineapple
2 tablespoons (2$\frac{1}{2}$ T) brown sugar
$\frac{1}{2}$ teaspoon salt
4 pineapple rings
1 onion
1 red pepper

Cut the spareribs into individual ribs, chopping through the bone if necessary. Half fill a large saucepan with water, add 4 tablespoons of the vinegar and bring to the boil. Add the spareribs and simmer for 20 minutes. Drain.

Place the cornflour (cornstarch), honey and soy sauce in a bowl and mix well. Coat the spareribs in this mixture. Heat about 1 inch of oil in a large frying pan and fry the spareribs until golden. Drain well on absorbent kitchen paper.

Put the pineapple syrup in a large saucepan with $\frac{1}{4}$ pint ($\frac{5}{8}$ cup) water, brown sugar, salt and the remaining vinegar. Bring to the boil, add the spareribs, cover and simmer for 30 minutes, turning occasionally. Add the pineapple and vegetables to the pan 5 minutes before the cooking time is finished.

Serve hot.

Serves 4-6

SWEET AND SOUR SPARE RIBS (*Photograph: Gales Honey*)

Beef with Broccoli on Noodles

$\frac{3}{4}$ lb. topside or rump steak
2 onions
4 oz. Chinese dried egg
   noodles
1 teaspoon very finely
   chopped fresh ginger
1 tablespoon (1$\frac{1}{4}$ T) soy sauce
1 tablespoon (1$\frac{1}{4}$ T) oil
1 teaspoon sugar

$\frac{1}{2}$ teaspoon salt
pinch of monosodium
   glutamate
pinch of pepper
2 tablespoons (2$\frac{1}{2}$ T) cornflour
   (cornstarch)
$\frac{1}{4}$ pint ($\frac{5}{8}$ cup) beef stock
8 oz. cooked broccoli
oil for deep frying

Cut the beef into thin strips about 2 inches $\times \frac{1}{4}$ inch $\times \frac{1}{4}$ inch.
Cut the onions into eighths. Cook the noodles in boiling water
for 5 minutes, then drain very well. Place the meat in a bowl,
add ginger and soy sauce and marinate for 30 minutes.
Heat the oil in a saucepan and fry the beef, stirring constantly,
until it has changed colour. Mix together the sugar, salt,
monosodium glutamate, pepper, cornflour (cornstarch) and
beef stock, stir well and add to the pan. Bring to the boil,
stirring, add the onions and simmer for 5 minutes. Add the
broccoli and cook 4-5 minutes.
Deep fry the noodles in hot oil until golden. Drain well on
absorbent paper.
Serve the noodles on a heated dish, topped with the beef and
broccoli.
Serves 4-6

Beef Chow Mein

$\frac{3}{4}$ lb. topside or rump steak
1 teaspoon salt
2 teaspoons sugar
1 tablespoon ($1\frac{1}{4}$ T) soy sauce
pinch of monosodium
   glutamate
4 Chinese dried mushrooms
1 × 16 oz. can bean sprouts
$\frac{1}{2}$ × 5 oz. can bamboo shoot
4 spring onions (scallions)

2 tablespoons ($2\frac{1}{2}$ T) cornflour
   (cornstarch)
$\frac{3}{4}$ pint (approx. 2 cups) beef
   stock
3 tablespoons ($3\frac{3}{4}$ T) peanut oil
4 oz. Chinese dried egg
   noodles
oil for deep frying
1 egg, beaten

Cut the beef into long strips, about 2 inches × $\frac{1}{4}$ inch × $\frac{1}{4}$ inch.
Mix together in a bowl the salt, sugar, soy sauce and
monosodium glutamate. Marinate the beef in this for 30
minutes.

Soak the mushrooms in warm water for 20 minutes, rinse,
squeeze dry and slice, discarding the stalks. Drain the bean
sprouts, rinse in cold running water and drain again. Slice
the bamboo shoot into thin strips. Cut the spring onions
(scallions) into 1 inch lengths. Mix the cornflour (cornstarch)
and stock together.

Drain the beef and reserve any remaining marinade. Heat the
oil in a pan and fry the beef, stirring, for about 3-4 minutes.
Add the marinade and the stock and cornflour (cornstarch)
mixture. Bring to the boil, stirring constantly, add the
prepared vegetables and simmer for 5 minutes.

Cook the noodles in boiling water for 5 minutes, then drain
them very thoroughly. Deep fry just before needed in hot oil.
Drain well on absorbent kitchen paper.

Beat the egg with 1 tablespoon of water and pour into a
heated, lightly oiled omelette pan. Make a small omelette and
cut it into thin strips.

To serve, place the noodles on a heated serving dish, top with
the beef mixture and garnish with strips of omelette.

Serves 4-6

Beef with Vegetables

½ lb. topside or rump steak
1 × 5 oz. can bamboo shoot
6 water chestnuts
1 onion
2 sticks celery
1 carrot
2 oz. button mushrooms
1 teaspoon very finely
  chopped fresh ginger

1 tablespoon (1¼ T) sherry
1 teaspoon sugar
½ tablespoon soy sauce
1 tablespoon (1¼ T) cornflour
  (cornstarch)
2 tablespoons (2½ T) peanut oil
1 clove garlic
¼ pint (⅝ cup) beef stock
salt and pepper

Cut the steak into thin strips, about 2 inches × ¼ inch × ¼ inch.
Cut the bamboo shoot into thin strips and slice the water
chestnuts. Cut the onion into eighths. Slice the celery and
carrot diagonally. Cut large mushrooms in half. Mix together
the ginger, sherry, sugar, soy sauce and cornflour (cornstarch).
Heat the oil in a frying pan with the garlic. Fry the garlic until
browned, then remove. Fry the beef until it changes colour,
stirring constantly. Add the soy sauce mixture, stock,
prepared vegetables and seasonings. Bring to the boil, stirring,
and simmer for 5 minutes.
Serve hot.
Serves 4-6

Meat Balls with Pineapple

½ lb. stewing steak (chuck or
  blade)
1 onion
½ egg
salt and pepper
cornflour (cornstarch)
oil for deep frying
½ × 15 oz. can pineapple
  pieces

¼ pint (⅝ cup) syrup from
  canned pineapple
1 tablespoon (1¼ T) cornflour
  (cornstarch)
2 tablespoons (2½ T) vinegar
1 tablespoon (1¼ T) soy sauce
2 tablespoons (2½ T) sugar
green tops of 2 spring onions
  (scallions), chopped

Mince the steak and onion together. Beat the egg lightly and stir it into the meat. Season. Form the mixture into small balls and roll in cornflour (cornstarch). Deep fry them in hot oil until golden.

Place all the remaining ingredients in a saucepan and bring to the boil, stirring constantly. Add the meat balls and simmer, covered, for 5 minutes.

Serve in a heated dish.

Serves 4-6

Red Cooked Beef

2 lb. topside (round or chuck) steak (in one piece)
1 tablespoon ($1\frac{1}{4}$ T) oil
1 tablespoon ($1\frac{1}{4}$ T) soy sauce
1 tablespoon ($1\frac{1}{4}$ T) hoi sin sauce
1 teaspoon sugar
1 teaspoon salt
pinch of pepper

1 teaspoon finely chopped fresh ginger
1 clove garlic, crushed
2 spring onions (scallions), chopped
1 teaspoon sesame seeds
1 tablespoon ($1\frac{1}{4}$ T) sherry

Trim any excess fat from the meat. Heat the oil in a large saucepan and brown the meat all over. Add all the remaining ingredients and enough water just to cover the meat. Bring to the boil and simmer for 2-$2\frac{1}{2}$ hours or until very tender.

Carve the meat into thick slices and pour the gravy over.

Serves 6-8

Woolly Lamb

This unusual dish owes its name and spectacular appearance to the transparent noodles. If these are not available, substitute 4 ounces of Chinese egg noodles, which should be boiled in water for five minutes, drained and fried.

1 lb. lamb (leg or shoulder)
$\frac{1}{2}$ × 5 oz. can bamboo shoot
1 onion
1 carrot
2 Chinese dried mushrooms
2 tablespoons ($2\frac{1}{2}$ T) peanut oil
$\frac{1}{2}$ teaspoon salt

$\frac{1}{2}$ pint ($1\frac{1}{4}$ cups) chicken stock
1 tablespoon ($1\frac{1}{4}$ T) soy sauce
$\frac{1}{2}$ teaspoon sugar
2 tablespoons ($2\frac{1}{2}$ T) cornflour (cornstarch)
2 oz. Chinese transparent noodles
oil for deep frying

Cut the lamb into thin slices and the bamboo shoot into thin strips. Cut the onion into eighths and the carrot into wedges. Soak the mushrooms in warm water for 20 minutes, rinse, squeeze dry and slice, discarding the stalks.

Heat the oil in a saucepan and fry the meat until it changes colour. Pour off the excess oil and add the prepared vegetables, salt, stock, soy sauce, sugar and cornflour (cornstarch). Bring to the boil and simmer, stirring constantly, for 5 minutes. Loosen the transparent noodles and deep fry in hot oil until they puff up, in about 15 seconds. Drain well on absorbent kitchen paper.

Serve the lamb mixture on a heated serving plate, topped with the noodles.

Serves 4-6

Lamb with Bean Sprouts

$\frac{1}{2}$ lb. lamb (shoulder or leg)
1 × 16 oz. can bean sprouts
2 spring onions (scallions)
1 tablespoon (1$\frac{1}{4}$ T) soy sauce
2 tablespoons (2$\frac{1}{2}$ T) vinegar
2 tablespoons (2$\frac{1}{2}$ T) brown sugar

1 teaspoon very finely chopped fresh ginger
salt and pepper
1 tablespoon (1$\frac{1}{4}$ T) cornflour (cornstarch)
1 tablespoon (1$\frac{1}{4}$ T) peanut oi

Cut the lamb in very thin slices. Drain the bean sprouts, rinse under cold running water and drain again. Cut the spring onions (scallions) into $\frac{1}{2}$ inch lengths. Mix together the soy sauce, vinegar, brown sugar, ginger, salt and pepper, cornflour (cornstarch) and $\frac{1}{4}$ pint ($\frac{5}{8}$ cup) water.
Heat the peanut oil in a frying pan and fry the lamb, stirring, until it changes colour. Stir the cornflour (cornstarch) mixture and add to the pan with the spring onions (scallions). Bring to the boil, stirring, and simmer for 2-3 minutes. Add the bean sprouts and cook for a further 2-3 minutes. Serve hot.
Serves 4-6

Shredded Lamb with Onions

1 lb. lean lamb (shoulder or leg)
4 onions
1 clove garlic, crushed
1 tablespoon (1$\frac{1}{4}$ T) soy sauce
1 tablespoon (1$\frac{1}{4}$ T) dry sherry

$\frac{1}{4}$ pint ($\frac{5}{8}$ cup) chicken stock
1 tablespoon (1$\frac{1}{4}$ T) cornflour (cornstarch)
1 teaspoon salt
2 tablespoons (2$\frac{1}{2}$ T) peanut oil

Cut the lamb into long thin strips. Slice the onions into $\frac{1}{8}$ inch rounds. Mix together the garlic, soy sauce, sherry, stock, cornflour (cornstarch) and salt.
Heat the oil in a saucepan and fry the lamb until it changes colour. Stir the cornflour (cornstarch) mixture and add it to the pan with the onions. Bring to the boil, stirring, and simmer for 2-3 minutes. Serve very hot.
Serves 4-6

Spiced Lamb with Vegetables

$\frac{3}{4}$ lb. lamb (shoulder or leg)
1 egg
2 tablespoons ($2\frac{1}{2}$ T) cornflour
  (cornstarch)
oil for deep frying
1 red pepper
1 onion
2 sticks celery
1 × 5 oz. can bamboo shoot
1 tablespoon ($1\frac{1}{4}$ T) soy sauce
1 teaspoon hoi sin sauce
1 teaspoon very finely
  chopped fresh ginger
1 clove garlic, crushed
pinch of monosodium
  glutamate
extra 1 tablespoon cornflour
  (cornstarch)
salt

Cut the lamb into thin strips, about 2 inches × $\frac{1}{4}$ inch × $\frac{1}{4}$ inch.
Beat the egg and cornflour (cornstarch) together, add the lamb
and stir to coat. Drain off any excess egg, then deep fry the
meat until golden. Drain well on absorbent kitchen paper.
Cut the pepper into wedges and the onion into eighths. Drop
the pepper and onion into boiling water and cook 5 minutes,
drain. Slice the celery diagonally and the bamboo shoot into
thin strips.
Mix together in a saucepan, the soy sauce, hoi sin sauce,
ginger, garlic, monosodium glutamate, salt, the extra cornflour
(cornstarch) and $\frac{1}{4}$ pint ($\frac{5}{8}$ cup) of water. Bring to the boil,
stirring constantly, add the vegetables and simmer for 2-3
minutes. Add the lamb and reheat.
Serve in a heated serving dish.
Serves 4-6

Poultry

At least one, and often two poultry dishes are included in a
Chinese menu, chicken and duck being the most frequently
used. As the cooking time is usually very short, you should
buy young birds whenever possible. Sometimes, however, the
recipe requires that the bird be boiled prior to being
incorporated in the finshed dish, in which case it is sometimes
more economical to use a boiling fowl, which must then be
cooked for long enough to ensure that the meat is very tender.

Braised Chicken with Vegetables

A little finely minced barbecued pork is delicious added to this recipe, if available.

$1 \times 2\frac{1}{2}$ lb. chicken
3 tablespoons $(3\frac{3}{4}$ T) soy sauce
1 tablespoon $(1\frac{1}{4}$ T) dry sherry
  (optional)
$\frac{1}{2}$ teaspoon sugar
1 teaspoon salt
1 pineapple ring
1 small pepper
1 carrot
1 stick celery
3 water chestnuts
2 tablespoons $(2\frac{1}{2}$ T) peanut
  oil

2 cloves garlic, crushed
1 teaspoon very finely
  chopped fresh ginger
$\frac{3}{4}$ pint (approx. 2 cups)
  chicken stock
1 spring onion, sliced
4 oz. spinach, finely shredded
1 tablespoon $(1\frac{1}{4}$ T) brown
  sugar
$1\frac{1}{2}$ (2 T) tablespoons cornflour
  (cornstarch)

Joint the chicken and cut each joint in half to make 8 pieces. Mix together the soy sauce, sherry, sugar and salt. Rub this all over the pieces of chicken and leave for at least 20 minutes. Cut the pineapple into eighths and the pepper and carrot into wedges. Drop these into a small saucepan of boiling water, cook for 5 minutes, and drain. Cut the celery diagonally and slice the water chestnuts into thin rounds.
Heat the oil in a frying pan and add the garlic and ginger. Fry, stirring, for 2 minutes. Add the chicken pieces and brown them all over. Pour off excess oil, add the chicken stock, bring to the boil and simmer, covered, for 30 minutes. Add the pineapple and vegetables to the pan and continue cooking until the chicken is very tender.
Arrange the chicken on a hot serving dish. Mix the sugar and cornflour (cornstarch) with a little water and add to the cooking liquid. Bring to the boil, stirring constantly and cook for 2-3 minutes. Adjust the seasoning. Serve with the sauce poured over the chicken.
Serves 4-6

Chicken Chow Mein

1 × 2½ lb. chicken
¼-inch slice fresh ginger
8 oz. Chinese dried egg noodles
1 onion
2 tablespoons (2½ T) peanut oil
3 sticks celery, sliced
4 oz. button mushrooms
8 water chestnuts, sliced
1 × 16 oz. can bean sprouts
1 × 5 oz. can bamboo shoot, cut in strips
1 tablespoon (1¼ T) cornflour (cornstarch)
2 tablespoons (2½ T) soy sauce
salt and pepper

Place the chicken and ginger in a large saucepan and add cold water to come halfway up the sides of the chicken. Bring to the boil and simmer until the chicken is tender, about 1 hour. Remove the chicken from the pan and reserve the stock.
Cut the chicken from the bones and cut the flesh into strips. Cook the egg noodles in boiling salted water for 20 minutes, or until softened. Drain well and keep warm.
Cut the onion into eighths. Heat the oil in a large frying pan and fry the onion until softened. Add the celery and mushrooms and ½ pint (1¼ cups) of the reserved stock. Bring to the boil and simmer for 5 minutes. Add the water chestnuts, bean sprouts and bamboo shoot.
Mix the cornflour (cornstarch) with soy sauce and 2 tablespoons of stock and add to the frying pan. Bring to the boil, stirring constantly, and simmer for 1-2 minutes. Add the chicken and season to taste.
Serve hot on the egg noodles.
Serves 4-6

Chicken with Celery and Pineapple Sauce

1 × 2½ lb. chicken
2 sticks celery
3 pineapple rings
1 tablespoon (1¼ T) cornflour cornstarch)
1 tablespoon (1¼ T) soy sauce
½ teaspoon very finely chopped fresh ginger
4 tablespoons (5 T) pineapple
syrup (from can)
4 tablespoons (5 T) brown sugar
4 tablespoons (5 T) vinegar
salt and pepper
1 egg
extra cornflour (cornstarch)
oil for deep frying

Place the chicken in a large saucepan and cover with water. Bring to the boil then simmer until tender. (This will be about 1 hour for a young bird or 2-3 hours for a boiling fowl.) Drain and allow to cool.

Cut the celery into diagonal slices and the pineapple rings into wedges. In a saucepan, mix together the cornflour (cornstarch), soy sauce and ginger with 4 tablespoons of water, pineapple syrup and sugar. Bring to the boil, stirring constantly, stir in the vinegar and cook for 2 minutes. Remove from the heat and add celery and pineapple wedges. Season to taste.

Disjoint the cooled chicken and cut each joint in half to make 8 pieces. Beat the egg with the salt and pepper. Dip the chicken pieces in egg and then in cornflour (cornstarch). Shake off the excess cornflour (cornstarch). Deep fry the chicken in hot oil until golden.

Arrange the chicken on a serving dish. Reheat the sauce and pour it over the chicken pieces. Serve hot.

Serves 4-6

Chicken with Lychees

1 × 2½ lb. chicken
2 tablespoons (2½ T) soy
  sauce
1 tablespoon (1¼ T) brown
  sugar
3 tablespoons (3¾ T) cornflour
  cornstarch)
salt

1 onion
1 small pepper
2 Chinese dried mushrooms
1 × 11 oz. can lychees
2 tablespoons (2½ T) vinegar
2 tablespoons (2½ T) oil
1 clove garlic, crushed

Place the chicken in a large saucepan and add water to come halfway up the sides of the chicken. Cook until tender (about 1 hour for a young bird and up to 3 hours for a boiling fowl). Skin the chicken and remove the flesh from the bones. Cut the meat into 2-inch squares. Mix together 1 tablespoon of the soy sauce, brown sugar, 2 tablespoons of the cornflour (cornstarch) and salt. Add the chicken and marinate for 30 minutes.

Cut the onion into eighths and the pepper into wedges. Put these in a small saucepan of boiling water, cook for 5 minutes, and drain. Soak the mushrooms in warm water for 20 minutes, squeeze dry, and rinse, and slice thinly, discarding the stalks. Strain the lychees, reserving the syrup. Add enough water to this syrup to make ½ pint (1¼ cup) of liquid, and combine this with the vinegar and remaining soy sauce.

Heat 1 tablespoon of the oil with the garlic, fry until golden and then remove the garlic. Fry the mushrooms for 2 minutes, add the lychee syrup mixture, bring to the boil and simmer for 2 minutes. Mix the remaining cornflour (cornstarch) with a little water, add to the pan and boil, stirring, for 2-3 minutes. Season to taste.

Drain the chicken and deep fry in hot oil until golden. Drain on absorbent kitchen paper. Add the vegetables and lychees to sauce and reheat. Arrange the chicken on a warm serving dish and pour the sauce over.

Serves 4-6

Crisp Skin Chicken

This dish is eaten with the fingers so place finger bowls of cold water on the table.

1 × 2½ lb. chicken
1 tablespoon (1¼ T) vinegar
2 tablespoons (2½ T) soy sauce
2 tablespoons (2½ T) honey
1 tablespoon (1¼ T) sherry

1 teaspoon treacle
2 tablespoons (2½ T) plain flour
1 teaspoon salt
peanut oil for deep frying

Put the chicken into a large saucepan and add boiling water to come halfway up the sides of the chicken. Cover tightly and simmer until just tender, about 45 minutes to 1 hour. Drain, rinse under cold water and dry with kitchen paper.

Mix together the vinegar, soy sauce, honey, sherry and treacle. Brush this all over the chicken and then hang the chicken in an airy place to dry, for about 30 minutes. Brush over the remaining soy sauce mixture and hang again for 20-30 minutes. Mix the flour and salt together and rub well into the chicken skin. Fry in deep hot peanut oil until golden and crisp. Drain well on absorbent kitchen paper.

Chop the chicken into 8 pieces and serve warm with the following dips.

Cinnamon Dip: Mix together 1 tablespoon ground cinnamon, ½ teaspoon ground ginger, ¼ teaspoon each freshly ground black pepper and salt. Place in a small saucepan and heat until very hot, stirring constantly.

Pepper and Salt Dip: Mix together 1 tablespoon salt, and ½ tablespoon freshly ground black pepper. Place in a small saucepan and heat, stirring, until the salt begins to brown.

Hoi Sin Sauce
Guests dip the pieces of chicken into the dips which are served separately in small bowls.

Serves 4-6

CRISP SKIN CHICKEN IN PREPARATION (*Photograph: Gales Honey*)

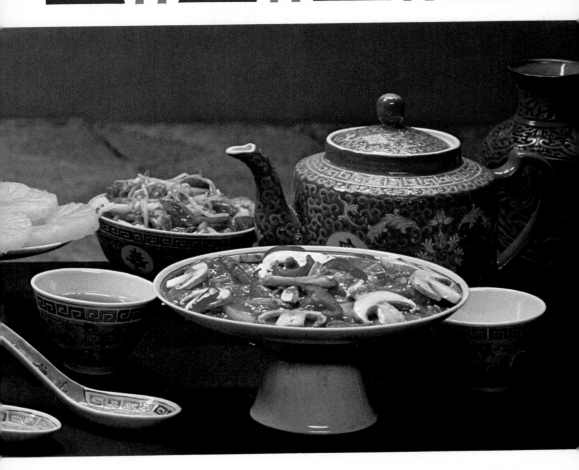

Chicken Salad

1 × 2 lb. chicken
1 teaspoon sesame seeds
1 teaspoon very finely
  chopped fresh ginger
2 tablespoons (2½ T) soy sauce
1 clove garlic, crushed
3 tablespoons (3¾ T) sugar
½ teaspoon five-spice powder

oil for deep frying
4 spring onions (scallions)
1 stick celery
6 water chestnuts
1 × 5 oz. can bamboo shoot
salt and pepper
6 lettuce leaves

Joint the chicken. Put the sesame seeds in a small pan and heat gently over a low heat, stirring, until they are toasted golden brown. Crush the ginger and mix with the soy sauce, garlic, sugar and ½ the five-spice powder. Pour this over the chicken and leave for 20 minutes, turning once.
Drain the chicken and fry it in deep hot oil until tender. Drain well on absorbent kitchen paper. Cool, then remove the meat from the bones and cut it into strips. Chill.
Cut the spring onions (scallions) into 1 inch lengths, slice the celery and water chestnuts and cut the bamboo shoot into thin matchstick strips. Mix the chicken with the rest of the five-spice powder and the vegetables. Toss all together lightly. Season. Line a mixing bowl with lettuce leaves. Place the chicken salad in the bowl and sprinkle with a little oil and the toasted sesame seeds.
Serves 4

Satin Chicken

1 × 4 lb. chicken
1 × 5 oz. can bamboo shoot
2 tablespoons (2½ T) soy sauce
2 cloves star anise
1 tablespoon (1¼ T) sherry
½ teaspoon salt
1 teaspoon very finely

  chopped fresh ginger
1 clove garlic, crushed
2 tablespoons (2½ T) peanut oil
¼ pint (⅝ cup) chicken stock
1 tablespoon (1¼ T) cornflour
  (cornstarch)
½ teaspoon sugar

PORK WITH CHICKEN AND VEGETABLES. CHICKEN CHOP SUEY ON BOILED RICE

Joint the chicken. Slice the bamboo shoot thinly.

Mix together the soy sauce, star anise, sherry, salt, ginger and garlic. Rub this mixture all over the chicken pieces and marinate for 1-2 hours.

Heat the oil in a saucepan. Add the chicken pieces and brown them well all over. Add the bamboo shoot and stock. Cover and cook for 20-30 minutes or until the chicken is very tender. Remove the chicken from the bones and cut the meat into long shreds. Mix the cornflour (cornstarch) and sugar with 3 tablespoons ($\frac{1}{4}$ cup) water. Add to the saucepan, bring to the boil, stirring, and simmer for 2-3 minutes. Return the chicken to the saucepan and reheat. Serve in a heated serving bowl.

Serves 4-6

Chicken Chop Suey

4 Chinese dried mushrooms
1 × 5 oz. can bamboo shoot
1 onion
1 pepper
1 × 16 oz. can bean sprouts
12 oz. (3 cups) cooked chicken
2 tablespoons ($2\frac{1}{2}$ T) peanut oil
$\frac{1}{2}$ pint ($1\frac{1}{4}$ cups) chicken stock
$\frac{1}{2}$ teaspoon sugar
1 teaspoon soy sauce
salt and pepper to taste
1 teaspoon cornflour
(cornstarch)
1 tablespoon ($1\frac{1}{4}$ T) dry sherry

Soak the mushrooms in warm water for 20 minutes, rinse, squeeze dry and cut into thin slices, discarding the stalks. Cut the bamboo shoot into thin strips. Cut the onion into eighths. Slice pepper thinly. Drain the bean sprouts, rinse in cold running water and drain again. Cut the chicken into $\frac{1}{2}$ inch cubes.

Heat the oil in a saucepan and add the chicken and vegetables. Cook, stirring, for 3-4 minutes. Add the stock, sugar, soy sauce and seasonings, bring to the boil, stirring constantly, and simmer for 5 minutes. Mix the cornflour (cornstarch) with sherry and add to the saucepan. Bring to the boil, stirring constantly, and cook for a further 3 minutes.

Serve hot.

Serves 4-6

Sweet and Sour Chicken Drumsticks

6 chicken drumsticks
1 egg
4 tablespoons (5 T) cornflour
  (cornstarch)
salt and pepper
1 onion
1 small pepper
1 carrot
¾ pint (approx. 2 cups)
  chicken stock

4 tablespoons (5 T) vinegar
4 tablespoons (5 T) soft brown
  sugar
1 tablespoon (1¼ T) cornflour
  (cornstarch)
1 tablespoon (1¼ T) soy sauce
1 tablespoon (1¼ T) sherry
  (optional)
oil for deep frying

Trim the drumsticks if necessary. Beat the egg with 1
tablespoon of water. Mix the cornflour (cornstarch) with salt
and pepper. Dip the drumsticks in egg, then in cornflour
(cornstarch) and put to one side.

Cut the onion into eighths and the pepper and carrot into
wedges. Drop these into a small saucepan of boiling water and
cook for 5 minutes. Drain well. Mix together, in a small
saucepan, the chicken stock, vinegar, sugar, cornflour
(cornstarch), soy sauce and sherry. Bring to the boil, stirring
constantly, and simmer for 2-3 minutes.

Heat the oil in a deep frying pan and fry the chicken drumsticks until golden and tender. Drain on absorbent kitchen
paper. Add the vegetables to the sauce and then add the
chicken. Reheat. Serve hot.

Serves 6

Chicken Wings with Mushrooms

2 tablespoons (2½ T) soy sauce
1 teaspoon salt
12 chicken wings
1 teaspoon finely chopped
  fresh ginger
6 Chinese dried mushrooms
4 tablespoons (5 T) peanut oil
8 oz. snow peas
2 spring onions (scallions),
  sliced

1 tablespoon (1¼ T) sherry
pinch of sugar
pinch of monosodium
  glutamate
¼ pint (⅝ cup) chicken stock
1 tablespoon (1¼ T) cornflour
  (cornstarch)

Sprinkle soy sauce and salt over chicken wings and marinate
for 30 minutes, turning occasionally.
Soak the mushrooms in warm water for 20 minutes, rinse,
squeeze dry and cut into thin strips, discarding the stalks.
String the snow peas and cook, in their pods, in ½ inch of
boiling salted water for 5 minutes.
Heat the oil and fry the chicken until golden brown and tender.
Pour off excess oil. Add the mushrooms, marinade, onions,
sherry, sugar, monosodium glutamate and the chicken stock.
Bring to the boil and simmer for 3 minutes. Mix the
cornflour (cornstarch) with a little water and add to the pan.
Simmer, stirring, for 2 minutes. Add the snow peas and cook
for 1 minute.
Note: Snow peas are available from some green grocers or they
can be bought from Chinese food stores. They are sometimes
called 'mange-tout' as the pods are eaten as well as the peas.
If you cannot buy snow peas, broccoli may be used.
Serves 4-6

Chicken Livers with Almonds

1 lb. chicken livers
2 spring onions (scallions)
2 tablespoons (2½ T) soy sauce
2 tablespoons (2½ T) dry
  sherry
1 clove garlic, crushed
½ teaspoon very finely
  chopped fresh ginger
½ teaspoon salt

1 tablespoon (1¼ T) brown
  sugar
2 tablespoons (2½ T) peanut oil
1 × 5 oz. can bamboo shoot
2 oz. (½ cup) flaked almonds
plain flour
¼ pint (⅝ cup) chicken stock
1 tablespoon (1¼ T) cornflour
  (cornstarch)

Remove any sinews from the livers. Put them into a small
saucepan of boiling water and cook for 2 minutes. Drain.
Chop the spring onions (scallions) finely and put them into a
bowl with soy sauce, sherry, garlic, ginger, salt and brown
sugar. Add the chicken livers, stir and marinate for 1-2 hours.
Drain the chicken livers and reserve the marinade.
Heat the oil in a frying pan and fry the bamboo shoot and the
almonds, stirring constantly, until the almonds are golden.
Remove and drain well. Coat the chicken livers in flour and
fry gently, stirring, until they are golden all over. Remove
from the pan. Mix the marinade, stock and cornflour
(cornstarch) in the frying pan. Bring to the boil, stirring, and
simmer for 2-3 minutes. Return the livers to the pan and
reheat. Serve in a heated dish, sprinkled with the almonds and
bamboo shoot.
Serves 4-6

Duck with Pineapple and Ginger

1 × 4 lb. duck

3 tablespoons ($3\frac{3}{4}$ T) lemon juice

2 tablespoons ($2\frac{1}{2}$ T) treacle

2 tablespoons ($2\frac{1}{2}$ T) soy sauce

1 tablespoon ($1\frac{1}{4}$ T) sherry

2 spring onions (scallions), chopped

2 tablespoons ($2\frac{1}{2}$ T) chopped preserved ginger

2 tablespoons ($2\frac{1}{2}$ T) syrup from ginger

2 pineapple rings, chopped

$\frac{1}{4}$ pint ($\frac{5}{8}$ cup) syrup from pineapple

$\frac{1}{2}$ teaspoon salt

$\frac{1}{2}$ tablespoon cornflour (cornstarch)

Place the prepared duck in a roasting pan. Mix together the lemon juice, treacle, soy sauce and sherry in a small saucepan and heat gently until the treacle has melted. Put the spring onions (scallions) into the duck with 1 tablespoon of the treacle mixture. Spoon some of the remaining treacle mixture over the duck and roast in a moderate oven (350°F, Mark 4) until tender, about $1\frac{1}{2}$- $1\frac{3}{4}$ hours, basting frequently with the treacle mixture.

To make the sauce, mix all the remaining ingredients together in a small saucepan. Bring to the boil, stirring constantly, and simmer for 2-3 minutes.

Chop the duck into eighths, though the bone, and place on a serving dish. Pour the sauce over and serve hot.

Serves 4-6

Braised Duck with Sweet and Pungent Sauce

1 × 4 lb. duck
salt
1 clove garlic, crushed
3 spring onions (scallions), very finely chopped
3 tablespoons (3¾ T) soy sauce
2 tablespoons (2½ T) sherry
2 tablespoons (2½ T) honey

Sauce:
1 small green pepper
1 × 5 oz. can bamboo shoot
2 Chinese dried mushrooms
1 teaspoon finely chopped fresh ginger
1 clove garlic, crushed

2 tablespoons (2½ T) oil
¼ pint (⅝ cup) stock
2 tablespoons (2½ T) honey
¼ pint (⅝ cup) pineapple juice
2 tablespoons (2½ T) vinegar
1 teaspoon tomato paste
1 tablespoon (1¼ T) dry sherry (optional)
1 tablespoon (1¼ T) soy sauce
salt and pepper
2 tablespoons (2½ T) cornflour (cornstarch)
1 × 11 oz. can mandarin oranges
4 pineapple rings, chopped

Wipe the duck inside and out with a damp cloth and rub it all over with salt. Mix the garlic, spring onions (scallions), soy sauce and sherry together. Divide this mixture into 2 and mix honey into one half. Rub the outside of the duck with some of the honey mixture and allow to dry.

Place the duck on a rack in a roasting pan and pour the soy sauce (*not* the honey) mixture inside. Pour 2 inches of water into the roasting pan and cook the duck in a moderate oven (350°F, Mark 4) for 1¾-2 hours or until tender, with the flesh coming away from the bones easily. Add ½ pint (1¼ cups) of boiling water to the honey mixture and baste with this every 20 minutes.

Sauce: Cut the pepper into wedges and the bamboo shoot into thin strips. Soak the mushrooms in warm water for 20 minutes, rinse, squeeze dry and slice, discarding the stalks. Place the oil in a saucepan and fry the prepared vegetables with the ginger and garlic for 5 minutes. Add the stock and bring to the boil.

Add the honey, pineapple juice and vinegar, bring to the boil again and stir until the honey has melted. Stir in the tomato paste, sherry, soy sauce and salt and pepper to taste. Mix the cornflour (cornstarch) with a little water and add to the pan. Bring to the boil, stirring constantly and simmer for 2-3 minutes.

Garnish the duck with the mandarin orange segments and pineapple wedges. Pour the sauce over the duck and serve hot.

Note: Make the stock from the duck giblets or use a chicken stock cube.

Serves 4-6

Crisp Duck with Five Spices

Supply finger bowls of cold water as this dish is eaten with the fingers.

1 × 4 lb. duck
2 tablespoons (2½ T) soy sauce
2 cloves star anise
1 teaspoon salt
1 tablespoon (1¼ T) brown
   sugar
2 teaspoons five-spice powder
1 tablespoon (1¼ T) salted

black beans
1 tablespoon (1¼ T) sherry
1 tablespoon (1¼ T) cornflour
   (cornstarch)
1 tablespoon (1¼ T) plain flour
peanut oil for deep frying
fruit chutney for serving

Place the duck in a large saucepan and add 1½ pints (3¾ cups) of water, the soy sauce, star anise, salt, and brown sugar. Bring to the boil and simmer until tender, about 2 hours. Drain the duck well and dry with absorbent kitchen paper. Mix the five spice powder with the beans and sherry and mash very thoroughly. Place 1 teaspoon of the mixture inside the duck and rub the rest over the outside. Sift the flours together and pat on to the outside of the duck. Deep fry the duck in hot oil until golden and crisp. Drain well on kitchen paper.

Chop into eighths through the bones and serve warm with a fruit chutney.

Serves 4-6

Eggs

Eggs are popular in China and are cooked in a very wide variety of ways. Egg dishes have always been a great favourite in Chinese restaurants and are extremely simple to cook at home. Besides being served as part of a meal, they are ideal for unusual supper dishes and snacks.

Prawn (Shrimp) Omelettes

This dish is good served as part of a meal, as an appetizer before the main course or simply as a snack. It can also be made as one large omelette and cut into serving pieces.

4 eggs
1 spring onion (scallion)
2 oz. ($\frac{1}{2}$ cup) prawns (shrimps)
salt
pinch of monosodium
   glutamate

6 fl. oz. ($\frac{3}{4}$ cup) chicken stock
oil for frying
1 tablespoon ($1\frac{1}{4}$ T) soy sauce
1 tablespoon ($1\frac{1}{4}$ T) cornflour
   (cornstarch)
1 teaspoon sugar

Beat the eggs and chop the spring onion (scallion) finely. Mix the eggs with the prawns (shrimps), onion, pinch of salt, monosodium glutamate and 2 tablespoons of the chicken stock. Heat a little oil in a small pan, add $\frac{1}{4}$ of the mixture and fry until golden underneath, stirring occasionally with a fork. Fold in half and keep warm on a plate. Make 3 more omelettes. Place all the remaining ingredients in a saucepan, bring to the boil, stirring constantly, and simmer for 2-3 minutes. Pour the sauce over the omelette and serve immediately.
Serves 4

PRAWN CHOP SUEY. SWEET AND SOUR PRAWNS. PRAWN OMELETTE (*Photograph: Young's Seafoods*)

Egg Pouch Omelettes

¼ lb. (1 cup) minced (ground) cooked pork
4 spring onions (scallions), finely chopped
1 tablespoon (1¼ T) soy sauce
salt, pepper
1 tablespoon (1¼ T) peanut oil
½ teaspoon sugar
½ teaspoon very finely chopped fresh ginger
1 tablespoon (1¼ T) cornflour (cornstarch)

1 tablespoon (1¼ T) sherry (optional)
4 eggs
oil
¼ pint (⅝ cup) chicken stock
1 extra tablespoon (1¼ T) soy sauce
1 extra tablespoon (1¼ T) cornflour (cornstarch)

Mix together in a bowl the pork, spring onions (scallions), soy sauce, salt, pepper, peanut oil, sugar, ginger, cornflour (cornstarch) and sherry. Beat the eggs.
Heat a little oil in a small omelette pan, pour in a large tablespoon of beaten egg and make a small plain omelette. While the egg is still moist on top, put a teaspoon of the pork mixture in the middle, fold the omelette over and press the edges lightly together. Remove to a serving dish and keep hot. Continue cooking in this way until all the egg is used. Place the chicken stock, and extra soy sauce and cornflour (cornstarch) in a small saucepan. Bring to the boil, stirring, and simmer for 2-3 minutes. Pour over the omelettes and serve immediately.
Serves 4-6

Eggs and Scallops

This dish is suitable for serving as an appetizer as well as part of the main course.

8 oz. scallops
½ × 16 oz. can bean sprouts
3 spring onions (scallions)

5 eggs
salt and pepper
1 tablespoon (1¼ T) peanut oil

Cut the scallops into small pieces. Drain the bean sprouts, rinse under cold running water, and drain again. Chop the spring onions (scallions) finely. Beat the eggs and season them. Heat the oil in a small frying pan, add the scallops and cook gently for 2-3 minutes. Add the eggs and cook quickly, stirring with a fork occasionally, until just set. Sprinkle the spring onions (scallions) on top and serve, folded, on a heated dish.
Serves 4-6

Mixed Omelette

3 eggs
$\frac{1}{2}$ teaspoon salt
2 tablespoons (2$\frac{1}{2}$ T) cooked or frozen peas
1 red pepper
2 spring onions (scallions)

1 tablespoon (1$\frac{1}{4}$ T) peanut oil
$\frac{1}{4}$ lb. ($\frac{1}{2}$ cup) minced lean pork
$\frac{1}{2}$ tablespoon dry sherry, optional
$\frac{1}{2}$ tablespoon soy sauce
pinch of sugar

Beat the eggs with salt and add the peas. Cut the pepper into matchstick strips and cook in boiling water for 5 minutes. Cut the spring onions (scallions) into thin slices. Add the pepper and spring onions (scallions) to the eggs.
Heat the oil in a frying pan, add the pork and cook, stirring until the colour changes. Pour the eggs into the pan, cook for 1 minute, and add the sherry, soy sauce and sugar. Continue cooking until the omelette is cooked but still moist on top. Serve immediately, on a heated serving dish.
Serves 4-6

Liang-Far Eggs

2 Chinese dried mushrooms
4 oz. Chinese cabbage or spinach
4 sticks celery
1 × 5 oz. can bamboo shoot
2 teaspoons soy sauce
1 tablespoon (1¼ T) dry sherry
½ teaspoon sugar
¼ pint (⅝ cup) chicken stock
1 tablespoon (1¼ T) cornflour
   (cornstarch)

pinch of monosodium
   glutamate
oil for frying
1 clove garlic, crushed
½ teaspoon salt
6 eggs
lettuce for serving

Soak the mushrooms in warm water for 20 minutes, rinse, squeeze dry and slice thinly, discarding the stalks. Shred the cabbage finely. Cut the celery diagonally. Cut the bamboo shoot into thin strips. Mix together the soy sauce, sherry, sugar, stock, cornflour (cornstarch) and monosodium glutamate. Heat 1 tablespoon of oil in a saucepan with the garlic and salt. Add the prepared vegetables and continue cooking, stirring, for 2-3 minutes. Stir the cornflour (cornstarch) mixture and add to the pan. Bring to the boil, stirring constantly, and simmer for 2-3 minutes. Keep hot.

Heat about one inch of oil in a small frying pan. Fry the eggs. Arrange the lettuce on a serving dish, put the eggs on top and pour the sauce over. Serve immediately.

Serves 6

Egg Rolls (Spring Rolls)

The filling can be varied – try substituting bean sprouts (rinsed in cold water and drained) instead of cabbage and prawns (shrimps) (finely chopped) instead of pork.

4 Chinese dried mushrooms
2 spring onions (scallions)
4 water chestnuts
4 oz. finely shredded Chinese
   cabbage or spinach
peanut oil
4 oz. ($\frac{1}{2}$ cup) minced (ground)
   lean pork

4 oz. (1 cup) minced (ground)
   cooked chicken
cornflour (cornstarch)
1 teaspoon soy sauce
4 oz. (1 cup) plain flour
pinch of salt
1 egg
oil for deep frying

Soak the mushrooms in warm water for 20 minutes, rinse, squeeze dry and chop very finely, discarding the stalks. Chop the spring onions (scallions) and water chestnuts finely. Cook the cabbage in 2 tablespoons of boiling water for 2 minutes and drain very well. Heat 1 tablespoon ($1\frac{1}{4}$ T) peanut oil and fry the pork, mushrooms and spring onions (scallions), stirring constantly, for 5 minutes. Add the chicken, water chestnuts, cabbage, 1 teaspoon of cornflour (cornstarch) and soy sauce and mix very well. Put aside to get cold.

Sift 2 oz. ($\frac{1}{2}$ cup) cornflour (cornstarch), plain flour and salt into a mixing bowl. Make a well in the centre and drop in the egg. Using a wooden spoon, mix a little flour into the egg. Gradually add 7 fl. oz. ($\frac{7}{8}$ cup) of water, slowly mixing in the flour. Beat well.

Heat a little oil in a small 6 or 7 inch omelette pan. Pour in enough batter to make a thin layer, cook on one side only then remove to a plate. Continue making pancakes until all the batter is used. Stack the pancakes one on top of the other. Divide the filling between the pancakes, placing it on the cooked side. Roll up the pancakes and tuck in the ends firmly. Seal them well with a cornflour (cornstarch) and water paste. Deep fry in hot oil until golden and drain well on absorbent kitchen paper. Serve piled onto a hot serving plate.
Serves 6-8

Prawn (Shrimp) and Mushroom Omelette

4 oz. (1 cup) peeled prawns (shrimps)
4 Chinese dried mushrooms
$\frac{1}{2} \times$ 16 oz. can bean sprouts
$\frac{1}{2}$ teaspoon very finely chopped fresh ginger

1 tablespoon ($1\frac{1}{4}$ T) sherry
2 tablespoons ($2\frac{1}{2}$ T) chicken stock
salt and pepper
4 eggs
oil for frying

Chop the prawns (shrimps). Soak the mushrooms in warm water for 20 minutes, rinse, squeeze dry and slice thinly, discarding the stalks. Drain the bean sprouts, rinse in cold running water and drain again.

Mix together in a saucepan the ginger, sherry, stock and seasonings. Add the prawns (shrimps) and vegetables, cover the pan and heat very gently for 5-7 minutes.

Beat the eggs with 1 tablespoon of water. Heat a little oil in an omelette pan, add the eggs and cook, stirring with a fork, until almost set. Put the prawn (shrimp) mixture in the centre and fold the omelette over.

Lift carefully on to a heated serving plate and serve immediately.

Serves 4-6

Preserved Chinese Eggs

Chinese preserved eggs are sold in shops which specialize in Chinese foods. They look very unappetizing but can make an unusual addition to a Chinese meal or can be served as an appetizer before the main course.

The grey coating of clay and rice husks is cracked and carefully removed. The eggs are then cut into quarters lengthways and are good served with Chinese mixed pickles, soy sauce and finely chopped fresh ginger.

Sweet and Sour Eggs

4 water chestnuts
1 carrot
$\frac{1}{4}$ pint ($\frac{5}{8}$ cup) chicken stock
1 clove garlic, crushed
1 tablespoon ($1\frac{1}{4}$ T) peanut oil
2 tablespoons ($2\frac{1}{2}$ T) sugar
2 tablespoons ($2\frac{1}{2}$ T) vinegar

1 teaspoon tomato paste
$\frac{1}{2}$ teaspoon salt
1 tablespoon ($1\frac{1}{4}$ T) cornflour
  (cornstarch)
4 eggs
oil for frying

Slice the water chestnuts thinly and the carrot in wedges.
Mix together in a small saucepan the stock, garlic, peanut oil,
sugar, vinegar, tomato paste, salt and cornflour (cornstarch).
Bring to the boil, stirring constantly, then add the vegetables
and simmer for 4-5 minutes.
Beat each egg separately with 1 teaspoon of water. Heat a
little oil in a small omelette pan and make 4 omelettes, one
after the other. Fold the omelettes and place on a serving dish.
Pour the sauce over and serve immediately.
Serves 4

Steamed Eggs with Crab

6 eggs
$\frac{3}{4}$ pint (approx. 2 cups)
  chicken stock
1 teaspoon dry sherry

1 tablespoon ($1\frac{1}{4}$ T) soy sauce
$\frac{1}{2}$ tablespoon peanut oil
4 oz. (1 cup) chopped crab
salt and pepper

Beat the eggs and add all the other ingredients. Pour into an
oiled pudding basin and cover with greaseproof paper and
then a layer of aluminium foil. Tie down securely.
Place in a steamer over gently simmering water for 30-40
minutes or until set. (The tip of a knife when put into the egg
will come out quite clean.)
Serve on a heated dish.
Note: Try using other seafood in this recipe such as prawns
(shrimps) or scallops, instead of crab meat.
Serves 4-6

Vegetable Omelettes with Sweet and Sour Sauce

4 Chinese dried mushrooms
$\frac{1}{2}$ × 16 oz. can bean sprouts
3 sticks celery
2 spring onions (scallions)
4 eggs
1 tablespoon (1$\frac{1}{4}$ T) soy sauce
salt and pepper
2 tablespoons (2$\frac{1}{2}$ T) vinegar
1 tablespoon (1$\frac{1}{4}$ T) sugar
1 tablespoon (1$\frac{1}{4}$ T) tomato
    paste

1 teaspoon cornflour
    (cornstarch)
$\frac{1}{2}$ teaspoon very finely
    chopped fresh ginger
1 red pepper
2 pineapple rings
2 tablespoons (2$\frac{1}{2}$ T) syrup
    from canned pineapple
oil for frying

Soak the mushrooms in warm water for 20 minutes, rinse, squeeze dry and slice thinly, discarding the stalks. Drain the bean sprouts, rinse in cold running water and drain again. Slice the celery diagonally and the spring onions (scallions) into thin rounds. Cook the mushrooms and celery in boiling water for 3 minutes, strain. Beat the eggs and add the soy sauce, salt and pepper, and prepared vegetables.

Mix together in a small saucepan the vinegar, sugar, tomato paste, cornflour (cornstarch) and ginger. Cut the pepper and the pineapple rings into wedges and add them to the saucepan with the pineapple syrup and 2 tablespoons of water. Bring to the boil, stirring constantly, and simmer for 3-4 minutes.

Heat enough oil to cover lightly the base of a small omelette pan. Add a generous tablespoon of the egg mixture and cook rapidly until lightly browned underneath. Place on a heated serving dish and keep hot. Continue cooking until all the egg mixture has been made into small omelettes. Pour the sauce over the omelettes and serve immediately.

Serves 4-6

Scrambled Eggs with Prawns (Shrimps)

4 eggs
8 oz. (2 cups) peeled prawns
(shrimps)
1 teaspoon chopped fresh
ginger
1 teaspoon dry sherry

1 teaspoon cornflour
(cornstarch)
pinch of monosodium
glutamate
pinch of salt
1 tablespoon ($1\frac{1}{4}$ T) peanut oil

Beat the eggs. Chop the prawns (shrimps) roughly. Crush the ginger with a knife blade and reserve the juice. Add the prawns (shrimps), ginger juice, sherry, cornflour (cornstarch), monosodium glutamate and salt to the eggs.
Heat the oil in a large frying pan, add the egg mixture and cook slowly until firm and lightly tinted underneath. Turn the eggs over and cook the other side until tinted brown.
Serve immediately on a heated dish.
Serves 4

Yellow Flow Eggs

2 Chinese dried mushrooms
5 eggs
2 oz. ($\frac{1}{2}$ cup) chopped prawns
(shrimps)
1 oz. ($\frac{1}{4}$ cup) chopped ham
1 oz. ($\frac{1}{4}$ cup) chopped bamboo
shoot

2 water chestnuts, chopped
1 tablespoon ($1\frac{1}{4}$ T) cornflour
(cornstarch)
1 teaspoon dry sherry
(optional)
pinch of salt
1 tablespoon ($1\frac{1}{4}$ T) peanut oil

Soak the mushrooms in warm water for 20 minutes, rinse, squeeze dry and chop mushrooms, discarding the stalks. Beat the eggs and add prawns (shrimps), ham, vegetables, cornflour (cornstarch), sherry, salt and $\frac{1}{4}$ pint ($\frac{5}{8}$ cup) of water.
Heat the oil in a saucepan, add the egg mixture and cook over a low heat, stirring continuously with a wooden spoon, until the eggs have set.
Serve on a heated serving dish.
Serves 4-6

Vegetables

Vegetables are often incorporated in the other savoury recipes in this book but they are also delicious served on their own, or as the main ingredient of a dish. They are always cut up into small pieces which cook very quickly and lend themselves to Chinese cooking methods. The Chinese never over-cook their vegetables – in fact to a Westerner they often appear to be under-cooked as they retain their colour and crispness. Chinese vegetables such as bean sprouts, bamboo shoot and water chestnuts are most easily obtainable canned. Some larger supermarkets, however, do stock some fresh Chinese vegetables – use these whenever possible.

Braised Cabbage with Mushrooms

1 lb. cabbage, or Chinese cabbage if available
2 tablespoons (2½ T) peanut oil
1 green pepper
1 tablespoon (1¼ T) soy sauce
1 teaspoon sugar
pinch of monosodium glutamate
4 oz. button mushrooms
salt and pepper

Clean the cabbage and chop it roughly. Heat the oil in a saucepan, add the cabbage and fry it for 2-3 minutes, stirring constantly. Cut the pepper into matchstick strips and add these to the pan with the soy sauce, sugar, monosodium glutamate and mushrooms. Season. Add 4 tablespoons of water, cover the pan and cook for 5-7 minutes, shaking the pan occasionally.
Put into a hot serving dish and serve immediately.
Serves 4-6

Bean Sprouts with Spring Onions

1 x 16 oz. can bean sprouts
2 spring onions (scallions)
1 tablespoon (1¼ T) peanut oil
1 clove garlic

¼ pint (⅝ cup) chicken stock
pinch of monosodium
　glutamate
salt and pepper

Drain the bean sprouts, rinse under cold running water and drain again. Slice the spring onions (scallions) into ½ inch lengths.
Heat the oil with the garlic and fry until golden. Remove and discard the garlic. Add the bean sprouts and onions to pan and fry, stirring continuously, for 3-4 minutes. Add the chicken stock and seasonings, bring to the boil and simmer for 2 minutes. Serve in a heated dish.
Serves 4-6

Braised Mushrooms

12 Chinese dried mushrooms
¾ pint (approx. 2 cups)
　chicken stock
1 tablespoon (1¼ T) soy sauce
2 spring onions (scallions),
　chopped

1 teaspoon very finely
　chopped fresh ginger
½ tablespoon cornflour
　(cornstarch)

Soak the mushrooms in warm water for 20 minutes, rinse and squeeze dry. Remove and discard the stalks. Pour the chicken stock into a saucepan, bring to the boil, and add the mushrooms, soy sauce, spring onions (scallions) and ginger. Cover and simmer for 1-1½ hours or until the mushrooms are very tender.
Put the mushrooms on to a serving plate and keep them warm. Mix the cornflour (cornstarch) to a paste with a little water and add it to the liquor in pan. Bring to the boil, stirring constantly, and simmer for 2-3 minutes. Pour the sauce over the mushrooms and serve.
Serves 4

Broccoli with Pork

12 oz. cooked or frozen
  broccoli
2 tablespoons (2½ T) peanut oil
1 teaspoon sugar
pinch of salt
½ teaspoon very finely
  chopped fresh ginger
1 clove garlic, crushed
2 tablespoons (2½ T) soy sauce
1 tablespoon (1¼ T) sherry
1 teaspoon cornflour
  (cornstarch)
¼ lb. (1 cup) thinly sliced
  cooked pork

Cut the broccoli into 1½ inch lengths. Heat the oil in a saucepan, add the broccoli and fry for 2-3 minutes. Add the sugar, salt, ginger and garlic, cover the pan and cook slowly for 4-5 minutes.

Mix the soy sauce, sherry and cornflour (cornstarch) with 3 tablespoons of water. Stir this in to the saucepan, cover again and cook for a further 3-4 minutes. Add the pork and reheat.

Serves 4-6

Vegetables with Sweet and Sour Sauce

1 small red pepper
1 small green pepper
1 onion
1 carrot
2 sticks celery
1 tablespoon (1¼ T) cornflour
  (cornstarch)
1 tablespoon (1¼ T) soy sauce
4 tablespoons (5 T) brown
  sugar
¼ pint (⅝ cup) chicken stock
4 tablespoons (5 T) vinegar
salt

Cut the peppers into wedges, the onion into eighths and the carrot into wedges. Slice the celery diagonally. Drop the vegetables into boiling water and simmer for 5 minutes.

Mix the cornflour (cornstarch) with the soy sauce. Put the sugar, stock and vinegar into a saucepan, bring to the boil and add cornflour (cornstarch) and soy sauce. Simmer, stirring, for 2-3 minutes. Add the vegetables and salt to taste and reheat. Serve in a heated bowl.

Serves 4

Sesame and Chicken Salad

1 × 11 oz. can lychees in syrup
6 lettuce leaves or Chinese
    cabbage leaves if available
3 tablespoons (3¾ T) peanut oil
2 tablespoons (2½ T) vinegar
1 tablespoon (1¼ T) toasted
    sesame seeds
1 teaspoon soy sauce
1 teaspoon sugar
pinch of monosodium
    glutamate
½ teaspoon dry mustard
salt and pepper
½ × 5 oz. can bamboo shoot,
    sliced
6 water chestnuts, sliced
3 spring onions (scallions),
    chopped
4 oz. (1 cup) cooked chicken,
    cut in thin strips

Drain the canned lychees. Shred the lettuce and put it in a covered bowl in the refrigerator to get crisp.

Mix together in a bowl the oil, vinegar, sesame seeds, soy sauce, sugar, monosodium glutamate, mustard, salt and pepper. Add the bamboo shoot, water chestnuts and spring onions (scallions) and marinate for 1 hour. Add the lychees and lettuce just before serving, toss lightly and put into a serving bowl. Scatter the chicken strips on top.

Note: Toast sesame seeds by placing them in a dry frying pan and heating very gently, stirring, until golden.

Serves 4-6

Mixed Vegetables

¼ pint (⅝ cup) chicken stock
pinch of sugar
pinch of monosodium
    glutamate
1 teaspoon soy sauce
2 teaspoons cornflour
    (cornstarch)
salt and pepper
2 Chinese dried mushrooms
1 onion
1 small green pepper
1 carrot
4 water chestnuts
½ × 16 oz. can bean sprouts
2 sticks celery
4 tablespoons (5 T) peanut oil

Soak the mushrooms in warm water for 20 minutes, rinse, squeeze dry and slice thinly, discarding the stalks. Cut the onion into eighths and the pepper and carrot into wedges. Slice the water chestnuts. Drain the bean sprouts, rinse in cold running water and drain again. Cut the celery diagonally. Heat the oil in a large frying pan, add the vegetables and fry gently for 5-7 minutes, stirring constantly. Add all the remaining ingredients and bring to the boil, stirring. Simmer for 2-3 minutes. Serve in a heated dish.
Serves 4

Stuffed Marrow

1 small marrow
4 oz. (1 cup) minced (ground) cooked pork
6 water chestnuts, chopped
$\frac{1}{2}$ × 5 oz. can bamboo shoot, chopped
salt and pepper
pinch of sugar
pinch of monosodium glutamate

beaten egg if necessary
$\frac{1}{4}$ pint ($\frac{5}{8}$ cup) chicken stock
1 tablespoon ($1\frac{1}{4}$ T) cornflour (cornstarch)
1 tablespoon ($1\frac{1}{4}$ T) soy sauce
1 tablespoon ($1\frac{1}{4}$ T) brown sugar
1 tablespoon ($1\frac{1}{4}$ T) vinegar

Peel the marrow, cut off one end and hollow out the centre by removing all the seeds. Mix together the pork, water chestnuts, bamboo shoot, salt and pepper, sugar and monosodium glutamate in a mixing bowl. Squeeze the mixture together, adding a little beaten egg if necessary to make the mixture stick together. Beat very well.
Stuff this filling into the marrow. Wrap the marrow in foil and place in a steamer over gently boiling water. Cook for 30 minutes or until very tender.
Place all the remaining ingredients in a small saucepan, bring to the boil, stirring constantly, and simmer for 2-3 minutes. Slice the marrow into 1 inch wide slices, place on a serving dish and pour the sauce over. Serve immediately.
Serves 4-6

Rice and Noodles

Rice is the staple diet of the Chinese. It is eaten at every meal. Short-grained rice is most commonly used, but the long-grained rice is often preferred in the Western world. Originally, boiled rice was always served, and fried rice was just a way to use up the cold left-over rice, the next day. Fried rice has now become a dish in its own right with many delicious variations.

Dried noodles are readily available in larger supermarkets, but it is worthwhile, if you have time, either to make your own or to buy fresh noodles from a Chinese food store. The noodle paste can also ne used for making dumplings and wun tuns.

Plain Boiled Rice

10 oz. ($1\frac{1}{4}$ cups) rice   2 teaspoons salt
1 pint ($2\frac{1}{2}$ cups) water

Wash the rice very well in several changes of water. Place the water in a large saucepan with the salt. Bring to the boil, add the rice and bring to boiling point again, stirring with a fork all the time. Cover the saucepan and cook the rice very slowly for 20 minutes. Remove the lid, allow the steam to escape and serve in a heated serving dish.

Note: Do not lift the saucepan lid before cooking time is finished or the steam will escape and the rice will not cook properly. More boiling water will probably have to be added. Cooked properly, the rice will have absorbed all the water by the time it is cooked.

This quantity serves **4-6.** If less rice is required, the amount of water should be adjusted proportionately. Thus for 6 ounces of rice, the same method should be followed, using 12 fluid ounces ($1\frac{1}{2}$ cups) of water.

Fried Rice

6 oz. ($\frac{3}{4}$ cup) rice

1 oz. ($\frac{1}{4}$ cup) blanched almonds

1 × 1 oz. slice cooked ham

3 spring onions (scallions)

2 eggs

$\frac{1}{2}$ teaspoon salt

2 tablespoons ($2\frac{1}{2}$ T) peanut oil

1 tablespoon ($1\frac{1}{4}$ T) soy sauce

Boil the rice (see recipe page 108). Cool, cover and place in the refrigerator or in a cool place overnight.

Split the almonds in half and toast them lightly by placing them in the grill pan under a very hot grill for a few minutes until golden. Stir occasionally and watch that they do not burn.

Cut the ham into long thin strips and chop the spring onions into $\frac{1}{4}$ inch lengths. Beat the eggs and salt together well.

Heat the oil in a large frying pan. Add the egg and fry until it is half cooked. Add the rice (make sure that there are no lumps) and coat the grains in egg, stirring quickly. Keep stirring and turning the rice over and over. Add the ham and onions and sprinkle in the soy sauce. Fry for 3-4 minutes, stirring constantly.

Serve in a heated serving dish sprinkled with the almonds.

Serves 4-6

Party Fried Rice

6 oz. ($\frac{3}{4}$ cup) rice

1 × 16 oz. can bean sprouts

4 oz. (1 cup) peeled prawns (shrimps)

4 oz. (1 cup) cooked chicken

2 eggs

salt

2 tablespoons ($2\frac{1}{2}$ T) peanut oil

1 tablespoon ($1\frac{1}{4}$ T) soy sauce

Cook the rice (see recipe page 108). Cool, cover and place in the refrigerator or a cool place overnight.
Drain the bean sprouts, rinse under cold running water and drain again. Cut any large prawns (shrimps) in half and cut the chicken into strips. Beat the eggs with salt. Heat the oil in a large frying pan. Add the eggs and fry until half set. Add the rice and fry quickly, stirring constantly until the grains are coated in egg. Keep stirring and turning the rice over. Add the prawns (shrimps), chicken and soy sauce. Fry, stirring constantly, for 3-4 minutes.
Serves 4-6

Variations for Party Fried Rice Crab, Lobster or Tuna Fish

Omit the bean sprouts, prawns (shrimps) and chicken.
Use 6 oz. ($1\frac{1}{2}$ cups) of flaked crab, lobster or tuna meat, 3 chopped shallots and 2 tomatoes (skinned, deseeded and chopped).

Pork and Mushroom

Omit the bean sprouts, prawns (shrimps) and chicken.
Use 8 oz. (2 cups) of cooked pork, cut into thin strips, 4 Chinese dried mushrooms, soaked in warm water for 20 minutes, rinsed, squeezed dry, and sliced thinly, discarding the stalks, and 2 spring onions (scallions), chopped. (Whole button mushrooms, 2 oz., can be used instead of the dried mushrooms).

Wun Tun

Wun tun skins can be purchased from shops specializing in Chinese groceries. You can however use noodle paste, which should be rolled out thinly and cut into squares. Serve wun tuns as part of the main course with a pungent sauce if liked. They can also be served as an appetizer or a snack.

24 wun tun skins or ½ the recipe for noodle paste, see page 114
8 oz. (2 cups) cooked minced chicken
8 oz. (2 cups) peeled prawns (shrimps)
2 spring onions (scallions)
pinch of sugar
pinch of salt and pepper
pinch of monosodium glutamate
1 tablespoon (1¼ T) soy sauce
egg yolk
oil for deep frying

Mince or chop finely the chicken, prawns (shrimps) and spring onions (scallions). Add the sugar, salt and pepper, monosodium glutamate and soy sauce and mix thoroughly.

Divide this filling evenly between the paste squares. Spread the filling over each square and roll it up, like a Swiss roll, folding in the ends. Seal the edges with egg yolk.

Deep fry in hot oil until golden. Drain well on absorbent kitchen paper and serve as soon as possible with pungent sauce.

Pungent Sauce: Mix together in a small saucepan 2 tablespoons of sugar, 2 tablespoons of vinegar, 1 teaspoon soy sauce, ½ teaspoon very finely chopped fresh ginger, 1 teaspoon tomato paste, ¼ teaspoon salt, ¼ pint (⅝ cup) water and 1 tablespoon cornflour (cornstarch).

Bring to the boil, stirring constantly, and simmer for 2-3 minutes.

Note: Wun tuns when made by the Chinese are folded in a very complicated manner. This recipe and rolling of the wun tuns will save a lot of time and tastes very good.

Serves 6-8

Variations on Wun Tun
Pork and Mushroom Filling

Omit the chicken and the prawns (shrimps).
Use instead 12 oz. (3 cups) minced (ground) cooked pork and 6
Chinese dried mushrooms (soak mushrooms in warm water for
20 minutes, rinse, squeeze dry, discarding stalks, and fry for
2-3 minutes in a little peanut oil, before mincing).

Prawn and Vegetable Filling

Omit the chicken.
Use instead 4 oz. (1 cup) shredded spinach, 4 water chestnuts
and 2 sticks celery.

Steamed Dumplings

$\frac{1}{2}$ the recipe for noodle paste, see page 114.
Chicken and prawn (shrimp) filling
or pork and mushroom filling
or prawn (shrimp) and vegetable filling, see pages 112, 113.
Roll out the noodle dough and cut it into 4 inch diameter
rounds. Using any of the fillings mentioned above, place the
filling on the rounds and either fold over the dough to make a
semi-circle (like a turnover) or gather up the edges into a small
bunch on top. Whichever way you choose to make the
dumplings, seal the opening well with egg yolk.
Place each dumpling on a piece of greased greaseproof or
waxed paper and pack closely in one layer in a steamer or
heatproof bowl. Either place the steamer over gently boiling
water or place the heatproof bowl in a pan of simmering
water so that the water comes halfway up the sides. Cover
closely. Steam steadily for 25-30 minutes.

Noodle Paste

1 egg   pinch of salt
8 oz. (2 cups) plain flour

Sift the flour and salt into a mixing bowl. Make a well in the centre and add the egg. Using a round bladed knife, mix the flour into the egg and then add enough water to make a stiff dough. Knead the dough with the hand, very thoroughly.
Roll out the dough as thinly as possible on a lightly floured board. Use as required.
Wun Tuns: Cut into 2-3 inch squares and use with one of the recipes in this chapter.
Dumplings: Cut into 4 inch diameter rounds and use with the recipes in this chapter.
Noodles: Lightly flour the dough, roll up like a Swiss roll and slice into 1/16-$\frac{1}{8}$ inch slices. Unroll and hang over the back of a chair (on a clean tea towel) for about 20 minutes, to dry out.
For soft noodles, boil for 5-7 minutes in a large saucepan of boiling salted water.
For crisp noodles, fry in deep hot oil until golden and drain well on absorbent kitchen paper. There is no need to boil the noodles before frying as with bought dried noodles.

Szechuan Noodles

4 oz. (1 cup) peeled prawns (shrimps)

1 × 1 oz. slice ham

1 stick celery

$\frac{1}{2}$ teaspoon fresh ginger

2 oz. ($\frac{1}{2}$ cup) minced (ground) cooked pork

2 tablespoons ($2\frac{1}{2}$ T) peanut oil

2 tablespoons ($2\frac{1}{2}$ T) brandy

$\frac{1}{2}$ teaspoon hot chilli sauce

1 tablespoon ($1\frac{1}{4}$ T) tomato sauce

1 tablespoon ($1\frac{1}{4}$ T) soy sauce

1 tablespoon ($1\frac{1}{4}$ T) cornflour (cornstarch)

3 tablespoons ($3\frac{3}{4}$ T) chicken stock

salt and pepper to taste

8 oz. Chinese dried egg noodles or homemade noodles (see recipe page 114)

Chop the prawns (shrimps) roughly and cut the ham into thin shreds. Chop the celery and chop the ginger very finely. Mix

together the pork, celery, prawns (shrimps) and ham.
Heat the oil in a frying pan. Add the pork mixture and fry, stirring, for 3-4 minutes. Add the brandy, ginger, sauces, cornflour (cornstarch), stock and salt and pepper. Cook, stirring constantly, for 7-8 minutes. Keep hot.
Loosen the Chinese dried egg noodles and cook in boiling salted water for 15-20 minutes or until tender. Drain thoroughly. Arrange the noodles on a heated serving plate and top with the sauce. Serve immediately.
Serves 4-6

Wor Mein

8 oz. Chinese dried egg
  noodles or homemade
  noodles (see recipe page 114)
6 oz. pork
1 carrot
1 onion
2 Chinese dried mushrooms

2 tablespoons ($2\frac{1}{2}$ T) peanut oil
$\frac{1}{4}$ pint ($\frac{5}{8}$ cup) chicken stock
1 tablespoon ($1\frac{1}{4}$ T) cornflour
  (cornstarch)
1 tablespoon ($1\frac{1}{4}$ T) soy sauce
6 hard boiled eggs
salt

If using Chinese dried egg noodles, loosen these and cook in boiling salted water for 15-20 minutes or until soft. Cook homemade noodles in boiling salted water for 5-7 minutes. Drain the noodles well and keep hot.
Cut the pork into thin strips, the carrot into wedges and the onion into eighths. Soak the mushrooms in warm water for 20 minutes, rinse, squeeze dry and slice, discarding the stalks. Heat the oil in a saucepan; add the pork and fry until browned, stirring constantly. Add the vegetables, cover and cook very gently for 10 minutes.
Mix together the stock, cornflour (cornstarch), soy sauce and salt to taste. Add to the pan, bring to the boil, stirring constantly, and simmer for 1-2 minutes.
Arrange the noodles in 6 individual serving bowls. Place the pork mixture on top and serve, garnished with quarters of hard boiled egg.
Serves 6

Crispy Noodles with Chicken and Vegetables

8 oz. Chinese dried egg
   noodles or homemade
   noodles (see page 114)
3 tablespoons ($3\frac{3}{4}$ T) peanut oil
6 oz. ($1\frac{1}{2}$ cups) cooked
   chicken
2 Chinese dried mushrooms
2 spring onions (scallions)
1 tablespoon ($1\frac{1}{4}$ T) soy sauce
pinch of monosodium
   glutamate

pinch of sugar
$\frac{1}{2}$ teaspoon salt
$\frac{1}{2}$ × 5 oz. can bamboo shoot
2 sticks celery
1 carrot
2 tablespoons ($2\frac{1}{2}$ T) chicken
   stock
$\frac{1}{4}$ inch slice fresh ginger
1 teaspoon cornflour
   (cornstarch)
oil for deep frying

If using Chinese dried egg noodles, loosen them, and cook in boiling salted water for 10 minutes, and drain well. Home-made noodles do not need boiling. Stir in 1 tablespoon oil into the noodles. Cut the chicken into strips. Soak the mushrooms in warm water for 20 minutes, rinse, squeeze dry and slice thinly, discarding the stalks. Chop the spring onions (scallions) finely.

Mix the soy sauce, monosodium glutamate, sugar and salt in a bowl. Add the chicken and spring onions (scallions), stir, and leave for 20 minutes.

Cut the bamboo shoot into thin strips, slice the celery diagonally and cut the carrot into wedges.

Heat the remaining 2 tablespoons of oil in a frying pan with the ginger. Remove the ginger, add the prepared vegetables and fry for 5 minutes, stirring constantly. Add the chicken and stock, mixed with the cornflour (cornstarch). Bring to the boil, stirring constantly, simmer 2-3 minutes. Keep hot.

Deep fry the noodles in hot oil until crisp and golden. Drain well on absorbent kitchen paper. Serve the noodles in a heated serving bowl, topped with the chicken and vegetable mixture.
Serves 4-6

Desserts

The Chinese usually like to finish a meal with some fresh fruit. This may be lychees, loquats or longans, but melon, bananas, apples, pears and mandarin oranges are also eaten. For a feast or special occasion, however, there are some light desserts and biscuits which may be served to complete the meal.

Almond Cream with Chow Chow

Chow chow is Chinese preserved fruit which can be bought in shops specializing in Chinese groceries.

1 × 16 oz. can chow chow or mixed fruit salad
1 pint (2½ cups) water
1 oz. (4 tablespoons) gelatine

¾ pint (2 cups) milk
granulated sugar to taste
1 teaspoon almond essence

Chop the larger pieces of chow chow in half or drain the mixed fruit salad.
Place 4 tablespoons of the water in a cup and stand it in a saucepan of hot water. Shower the gelatine into the cup and heat, stirring, until the gelatine has dissolved. Cool.
Heat the remaining water with milk, sugar to taste, and almond essence, stir until the sugar is dissolved. Stir in the gelatine. Pour into a shallow, lightly oiled cake tin and cool until set.
Cut the almond cream into triangular bite-sized pieces. Place these in a serving bowl with the fruit and combine very gently. Serve very cold.
Serves 6-8

Almond Lake with Mandarin Oranges

1 pint (2½ cups) milk
4 oz. (½ cup) granulated sugar
1 teaspoon almond essence
2 oz. (⅓ cup) ground rice

1 × 11 oz. can mandarin
  oranges
1 oz. (¼ cup) flaked toasted
  almonds

Put the milk, sugar, essence and rice into a saucepan. Bring to the boil, stirring constantly, and simmer for 5 minutes. Pour into a dish, cover and cool. Drain the mandarin oranges well. Spoon the rice into individual serving dishes. Place the mandarin oranges on the rice and sprinkle the toasted almonds on top.
Note: Toast the almonds by placing in the grill pan and heating under a hot grill, stirring occasionally, until golden.
Serves 4-6

Gingered Fruit

1 × 15 oz. can pineapple pieces
1 × 11 oz. can lychees
1 tablespoon (1¼ T) chopped
  glacé cherries

2 tablespoons (2½ T) chopped
  crystallized ginger
1 oz. (¼ cup) toasted flaked
  almonds

Drain the syrup from the canned fruits. Lightly combine the pineapple, lychees, glacé cherries and ginger in a serving bowl. Chill well. Sprinkle the almonds on top and serve immediately.
Note: Toast the almonds by spreading the blanched, flaked almonds in the grill pan and heating them, stirring occasionally, until lightly tinted.
Serves 6-8

ALMOND LAKE WITH MANDARIN ORANGES (*Photograph: John West*)

Caramel Apples

Other fruit, such as bananas, pears, plums, can also be served in this way.

6 apples
1½ oz. (6 T) plain flour
½ oz. (2 T) cornflour
   (cornstarch)
2 egg whites

oil for deep frying
4 oz. (½ cup) granulated sugar
1 tablepsoon (1¼ T) oil
1 tablespoon (1¼ T) sesame seeds

Peel, core and quarter the apples. Dust them lightly with some of the plain flour.
Sift the remaining plain flour with the cornflour (cornstarch) into a mixing bowl. Add the egg whites and mix to a paste. Add the apple quarters and stir to coat in paste. Deep fry in hot oil until golden. Drain well on absorbent kitchen paper. Place the sugar in a small saucepan with 2 tablespoons (¼ cup) water. Heat, stirring, until the sugar has dissolved. Add the oil and continue heating slowly until the sugar has caramelised and is a light golden brown. Stir in the apple and sesame seeds. Serve immediately in individual serving dishes which have been very lightly oiled. A bowl of cold water should also be on the table and the guests pick up their apple with chopsticks or tongs and drop them into the water before eating, for the caramel to harden.
Serves 4-6

CARAMEL APPLES *(Photograph: The Fruit Producers' Council)*

Eight Treasures Rice

6 oz. ($\frac{3}{4}$ cup) short grain rice
4 oz. ($\frac{2}{3}$ cup) brown sugar
2 oz. ($\frac{1}{2}$ cup) dates
2 oz. ($\frac{1}{2}$ cup) blanched
    almonds
2 oz. ($\frac{1}{2}$ cup) walnuts

2 oz. ($\frac{1}{3}$ cup) glacé cherries
2 oz. ($\frac{1}{2}$ cup) mixed peel
2 oz. ($\frac{1}{2}$ cup) raisins
2 oz. ($\frac{1}{3}$ cup) glacé pineapple,
    apricots, or figs as available

Cook the rice in boiling water for about 15 minutes or until tender. Drain and stir in the sugar.

Place a layer of rice in the base of an oiled $1\frac{1}{2}$-2 pint pudding bowl. Add a layer of fruit and nuts to make a pattern, pressing it through the rice so that it will be seen as decoration when the pudding is unmoulded. Add another layer of rice, then a layer of mixed nuts and fruit. Continue layering until all the ingredients have been used, finishing with a layer of rice.

Press down very firmly and cover with greased greaseproof paper or aluminium foil. Place the bowl in a steamer over gently boiling water, or in a saucepan with simmering water coming halfway up the side of the bowl. Cook for 30-40 minutes. Unmould and serve hot.

Serves 6-8

Mow Flower Twists

8 oz. (2 cups) plain flour
4 oz. ($\frac{1}{2}$ cup) margarine or
  butter
4 oz. ($\frac{1}{2}$ cup) granulated sugar
1 oz. (3 tablespoons) ground
  almonds

1 egg
$\frac{1}{2}$ teaspoon almond essence
oil for deep frying
icing sugar

Sift the flour into a bowl and rub in the margarine or butter with the fingertips until the mixture resembles breadcrumbs. Stir in the sugar and ground almonds. Add the egg and essence and kead very well to make a pliable dough, adding a little water if necessary.

Roll the dough into a sausage about 1 inch in diameter and cut off 1 inch lengths. Roll each piece into a ribbon about 9-10 inches long, fold in half and twist twice. Take the ends of the ribbon back to the fold and push through the loop.

Carefully fry these twists in deep hot oil and cook until golden. Drain well on absorbent kitchen paper. Sprinkle with icing sugar. Serve cold.

Makes about 16

Sesame Biscuits

4 oz. ($\frac{1}{2}$ cup) granulated sugar $\frac{1}{2}$ teaspoon baking powder
4 oz. ($\frac{1}{2}$ cup) margarine or butter   8 oz. (2 cups) plain flour
                                                sesame seeds

Cream the butter and sugar in a bowl until light and soft.
Beat in 1 egg gradually, beating well after each addition. Stir
in the flour sifted with the baking powder.
Place the dough on a lightly floured board and knead lightly.
Form the dough into balls about 1 inch in diameter and flatten
with the palm of the hand.
Separate the remaining egg, beat the yolk lightly and brush it
over the biscuits. Press the egg yolk side of the biscuits into
the sesame seeds and press them on firmly.
Place the biscuits on a lightly oiled baking tray, seed side up,
brush with the egg white and bake in a moderate oven
(350°F, Mark 4) for about 15 minutes or until golden. Cool
on a wire cooling tray.   **Makes about 30 biscuits**

Almond Biscuits

12 oz. (3 cups) plain flour   1 egg
2 teaspoons baking powder   1 teaspoon almond essence
pinch of salt   blanched almonds for
4 oz. ($\frac{1}{2}$ cup) margarine or   decoration
   butter   beaten egg for glazing
8 oz. (1 cup) granulated sugar

Sift the flour, baking powder and salt into a bowl. Cream the
margarine and sugar together until light, white and fluffy.
Beat in the egg and almond essence. Stir in the sifted dry
ingredients to make a stiff dough.
Form the mixture into balls about 1-1$\frac{1}{4}$ inch diameter and place
these on a greased baking tray. Place half an almond (split
lengthways) on each ball and press to flatten slightly. Brush
with beaten egg.
Bake in a moderate oven (350°F, Mark 4) for 20 minutes or
until golden. Cool on a wire rack. **Makes about 45 biscuits**

Index